AMERICAN FOOTBALL

HOW TO WATCH AND PLAY

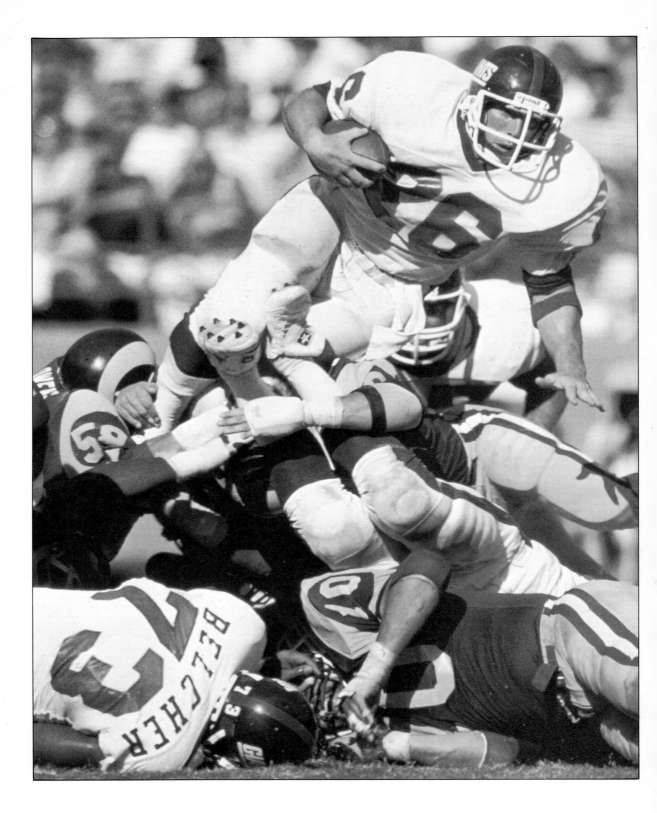

AMERICAN FOOTBALL
HOW TO WATCH AND PLAY

David Nelson and William E. Elstran

Stanley Paul
London Melbourne Auckland Johannesburg

This guide to American Football is dedicated to two very special groups of British men – those who took their game of football to the colonies some 300 years ago, and those who are now bringing the revised game back to Britain.

Stanley Paul & Co. Ltd

An imprint of Century Hutchinson Ltd
Brookmount House, 62–65 Chandos Place,
Covent Garden, London WC2N 4NW

Century Hutchinson Australia (Pty) Ltd
PO Box 496, 16–22 Church Street, Hawthorn, Melbourne, Victoria 3122

Century Hutchinson New Zealand Limited
32–34 View Road, PO Box 40–086, Glenfield, Auckland 10

Century Hutchinson South Africa (Pty) Limited
PO Box 337, Bergvlei 2012, South Africa

First published 1986

© David Nelson and William Elstran 1986

Set in 10 on 11.5 Helvetica
by Butler & Tanner Ltd, Frome and London

Printed and bound in Great Britain by Butler & Tanner Ltd,
Frome and London

British Library Cataloguing in Publication Data

Nelson, David
  American football: how to watch and play
  1. Football
  I. Title II. Elstran, Williams E.
  796.332   GV951
ISBN 0 09 166201 X

Contents

David Nelson

Dave Nelson's association with American Football spans over half a century. He played his first game in the year that Her Majesty the Queen's grandfather was celebrating his Silver Jubilee. Winston Churchill was on the 'back benches' and Margaret Thatcher, living above the shop, was 'warming up' with her first elocution lesson.

After four years of high school participation in Oregon, where he was an All-Conference player, Dave played for two small colleges in Oregon and Idaho. His twenty-three years of coaching includes experience in Oregon, Washington and California, as well as working with a US Air Force team and US Department of Defense School teams in England. In addition to coaching he taught history and also served as headmaster in international schools in Holland and Switzerland.

He was named Air Force Europe Coach of the Year in 1976 and UK American Schools Coach of the Year in 1981. Since 1984 he has been coaching the Plymouth Admirals and conducting clinics for newly formed teams in England.

Dr William E. Elstran

Bill's passing and running earned him the honour of being selected second team All-State High School at the position of quarterback. His play gained him a scholarship at the University of Wisconsin, Eau Claire. As the varsity quarterback for three years, he set a record for the university in pass completions.

His masters degree was earned at Stanford University and his doctorate at the University of Southern California. He has extensive experience in teaching physics and mathematics at both the high school and university levels. As director of ElSyd Educational Consultants, he has conducted numerous workshops in the United States and Europe on subjects germane to contemporary education.

During his eighteen years as player and coach his teams compiled a record of 103–37–4.

For the past fifteen years he has stayed with the game as an official, athletic director, or athletic co-ordinator. He is currently Athletic Co-ordinator for the American Department of Defense Dependents' Schools in London.

Opposite above: *Bill* (left) *and Dave*

Opposite below: *Nelson and the Admirals*

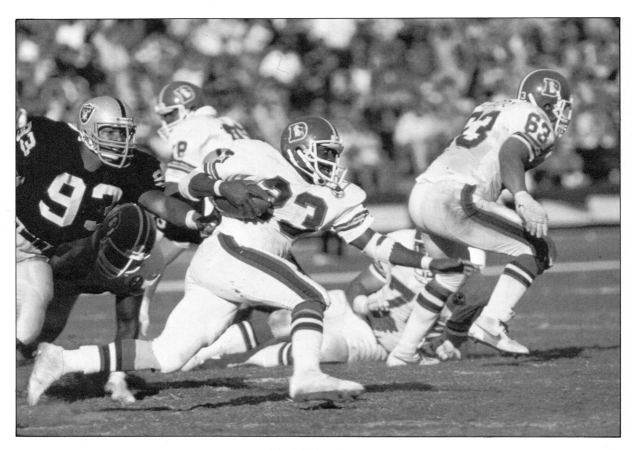

Turning the corner

Introduction

*For when the One Great Scorer comes to mark against
  your name,
He writes – not that you won or lost – but how you played
  the Game.*

GRANTLAND RICE
SPORTSWRITER

In the autumn of 1985, research indicates that 3·4 million British men (and some women) sacrificed golf, sex and gardening to watch American Football.

American Football is the fastest growing sport in Great Britain, for both spectators and participants. Some 12,000 British males have purchased their 'kit' and are 'banging heads'.

In January, 1986, the most modern of electronic capabilities transmitted, via satellite, the Super Bowl to England. The late Sunday night game ended at 3:15 a.m. It is estimated that 8·2 million employees arrived at work late that Monday morning. Fourteen per cent of those were women.

What is the Super Bowl?
Why were 14 per cent of the spectators women?
What happened to the gardening?
Will golf be banned on Sundays?
Is sex really on the decline?
When the 'quarterback takes the centre', does he
  take him to lunch?
Is a 'tight end' Terry Wogan at the end of a bar
  with his hand on his wallet?
When you have 'inside responsibility' is that
  the next Brinks Job?
Is a 'draw play' a poker hand with a chance for
  an inside straight?
Will a 'completed pass' get the quarterback in
  trouble with his wife?
Is a 'fair catch' a legal size trout?

This book will give you all the answers. When you get to the end, you should be able to watch a game, know who scored, who didn't score, and why and how it happened. The book will also give you a lot of insight into the game, making frequent references to past developments. When William 'The Refrigerator' Perry scored in Super Bowl XX, for example, he ran a basic 'dive play'. Yet the dive play is what made Stanford University a football power in 1940. On the other hand, newspapers may talk about the 'Refrigerator' today; next season they might refer to him as the 'Washing Machine' because a professional player can 'wash out' of American Football through an injury, contract dispute, or change in theory by one of the coaches.

This book is intended to serve as a reference for the TV viewer, the new player and even the coach. As American Football continues its spectacular growth it must be understood by spectators and prospective participants of all ages. This is why our book is not designed for the TV spectator alone. It

Aren't we nifty?

goes far beyond that, allowing for father to get off the cushions and show the game to his son in the back garden. Indeed, players at any level could benefit from the history, the development and the theory presented.

The game is rough but disciplined, well-organized and highly logical, going far beyond the showbiz, razzmatazz image projected on television screens. However, it cannot be fully appreciated until it is examined in simple, straightforward terms. In sports, as in many other areas, a tremendous amount of technical jargon is employed – perhaps to bolster egos and add an aura of intellectualism to something quite simple. Consequently the outsider could be confused and discouraged from becoming involved due to the 'closed shop' atmosphere. *American Football: How to Watch and Play* will clear up those esoteric terms. Use the text and diagrams as you watch the game on TV or go out on the field at your local club.

To understand and be involved in American Football it is necessary to know the basics,

appreciate the history and have a feel for the development of the game. The bulk of football literature published in Britain is concerned solely with professional teams. Yet, since the game evolved in the schools and universities, we need to trace its history and development with constant reference to the non-professional background. After all, it should be remembered that the vast majority of the spectators and participants in America are involved at the school and university levels. Professional football is only the tip of the iceberg.

Before we begin, here are a few quick tips on understanding the game, and an easy key to help you with the diagrams. So as not to confuse things, we'll stick to the American spellings for 'offense' and 'defense', to remind you of the right pronunciation with the emphasis on the first syllable. (It may also help you to remember that the *off*ense is *advancing* the ball and the *def*ense is trying to stop them.)

Perspective illustration of offensive and defensive alignment. Compare with diagram opposite

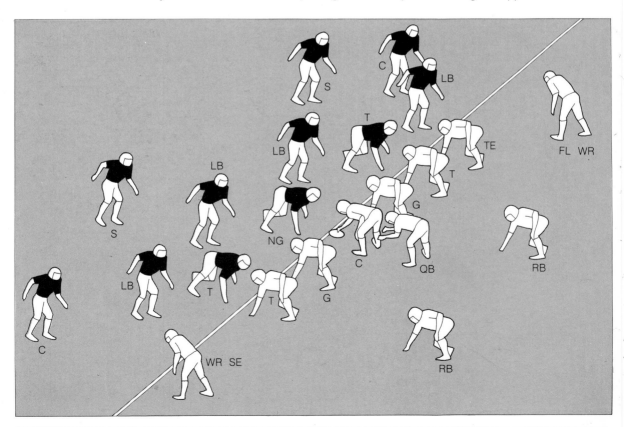

- The game consists of 'plays'. The offensive team meets in a group, called the 'huddle'. In the huddle they decide what they are going to do on their next 'play'. In fact, American Football has been described as a series of meetings (huddles) separated by violence!
- Following the huddle the teams assemble on a position on the field. This is called the 'line of scrimmage', perpendicular to the direction of the play.
- At any given time there are twenty-two players on the field. Eleven of them are on offense, trying to move the ball toward the goal. The other eleven are on defense trying to ensure that the offense is not successful.
- Throughout the book the diagrams will have a 'helicopter' perspective: in other words, you will be looking down from the sky on to the field.
- The *offensive* men will be represented as small circles or O's and the *defensive* men as triangles.

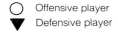

  ○ Offensive player
  ▼ Defensive player

- The ball is positioned on the field and handled by a man called the centre. He is identified by a circle with an 'X'.

  ⊗ Offensive centre

- At the start of each 'play' or action he will hand the ball, between his legs, to another player called the quarterback. Sometimes he tosses it between his legs to the quarterback if his team-mate lines up further back.
- The diagrams will show the man who has the ball for a portion of the play by filling in half of the circle.

  ◐ Player handling the ball for part of the play

- And the man who ends up with the ball at the *end* of the play is denoted with the circle being filled.

  ● Ball carrier or receiver

- You have to appreciate that the ball could change from player to player several times to add

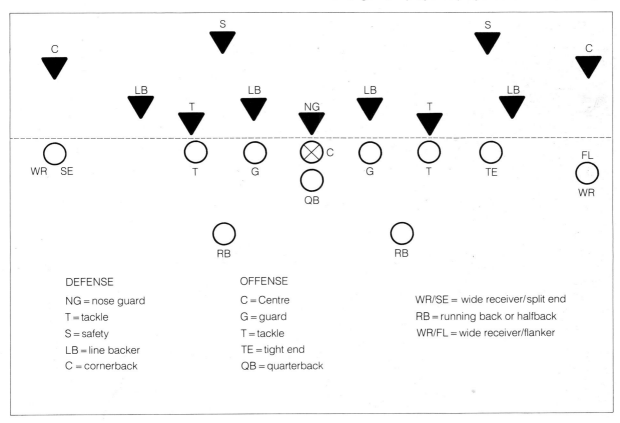

DEFENSE	OFFENSE	
NG = nose guard	C = Centre	WR/SE = wide receiver/split end
T = tackle	G = guard	RB = running back or halfback
S = safety	T = tackle	WR/FL = wide receiver/flanker
LB = line backer	TE = tight end	
C = cornerback	QB = quarterback	

deception to the play. Unlike rugby, there is a real effort to 'hide' the ball.

● At the start of each play seven of the offensive men must be on a line that is perpendicular to the direction of play (the line of scrimmage).

● Incidentally, we think the word 'scrimmage' is Latin and means 'beat the sin out the man on the opposite side of the line'. For sure it means 'little battle'. Regardless of the accuracy of the definition, in any case, the defense will have three to eight men opposite the offensive men and the rest of the eleven behind these. It will look something like this:

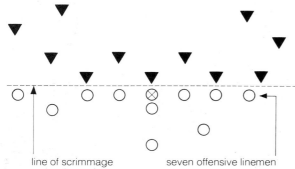

line of scrimmage   seven offensive linemen

● These offensive men on the line of scrimmage will try to 'block' the defensive men. In other words, they will try to use their bodies to knock the defensive men out of the path of their man with the ball. This is denoted in the diagrams like this:

where the offensive man (◯) throws a block on the defensive man (▼), so you can see clearly which side the block comes from.

We hope that this book will put your feet in the past, your head in the present and your heart in the future.

Welcome to the exciting world of American Football.

Opposite: *Heading for pay dirt*

Below: *The huddle*

'A streak of fire, a breath of flame
Eluding all who reach and clutch;
A grey ghost thrown into the game
That rival hands may rarely touch ...'

GRANTLAND RICE,
Writing about the famous Red Grange, thereafter
known as the 'Galloping Ghost'

1 History of the game

Although the origins of the game of American Football are, as the historians say, 'shrouded in the mists of antiquity', some clearly marked milestones remain.

The Greeks played Harpaston in which a ball was kicked, passed or carried across a goal line. The Romans, after conquering Greece, modified the game and called it Calcio. Roman troops probably introduced Calcio to Britain after the conquest of AD 43.

Danish invasions of the ninth century resulted in another interesting development which, even if not accepted as Gospel truth, must be mentioned. The invaders were so detested by the locals that they would exhume the body of a Danish casualty and use the head as a ball. This provided a healthy outlet for pent-up hatred, as well as a sturdy, inexpensive ball. The Roman name was dropped, and the game was known locally as 'Kicking the Dane's Head'. No records remain of the Danish reaction to this practice.

By the Middle Ages the game had become so popular and dangerously rough that royal attempts were made to outlaw it, but to no avail. Eventually some semblance of order was established, and football was introduced to public schools such as Eton, Harrow and Winchester. This tended to make the game socially acceptable, and it was no longer considered a barbarous diversion fit only for the lower orders of society.

English football was primarily a kicking game until 1823, when William Ellis of Rugby school picked up the ball and ran with it. This radical act eventually led to a completely new game called Rugby.

English colonists brought their game to America in the seventeenth century, and by the eighteenth century it had become popular with college students on the eastern seaboard. Rules were few and varied with the locality. A team consisted of between fifteen and twenty-five players, and scoring was accomplished by kicking, throwing, or dribbling the ball across the opponents' goal.

The very early American ball consisted of an inflated pig's bladder. This was later enclosed in leather, but the term 'pigskin' is still used in football vernacular when referring to the ball.

The year 1869 marks the beginning of interscholastic competition with a game between Princeton and Rutgers Universities. Each team employed twenty-five players who had no protective equipment but merely removed their hats, coats and vests before going into action.

In this formative stage, each school developed its own version of the game. There were no official rules until 1873, when representatives from Columbia, Yale, Rutgers and Princeton met to establish a code of rules governing contests between their universities.

Even though Rugby was becoming increasingly popular, American Football still resembled soccer more than any other game until 1876. In that year the American Intercollegiate Football Association was formed to play under Rugby rules.

From this time we see a very rapid development toward American Football as we now know it.

In 1879, running interference (blocking) for the ball carrier was introduced. During the 1880s the number of players on a side was reduced to eleven. The offense was now required to gain five yards in three downs (attempts), which led to lining the field at five-yard intervals and referring to it as the gridiron because of the pattern made by the lines. By the 1890s, rudimentary uniforms made of canvas were appearing. These early uniforms had little padding and no protection for the head.

The forward pass was introduced in the early 1900s, as well as a rule requiring the offense to gain ten yards in three downs or relinquish possession of the ball. The year 1910 saw the game divided into four fifteen-minute quarters. Seven men were now required on the line of scrimmage. In 1912 the field was set at 100 yards with ten-yard end zones. A touchdown earned six points, and the offensive team was given four downs to gain ten yards. A quick review of developments since 1900 will lead to the realization that by 1912 Football had become essentially the game we know in the 1980s.

All competitive activities from jousting to snooker have their heroes. American Football is no exception. Countless pages have been written on the immortals and many books are devoted to just one man. Interspersed in the text, therefore, are brief commentaries on some of the men who guided and shaped the game in its formative years.

It is not within the scope of this book to make Hall of Fame nominations, but homage must be paid to two famous names: Walter Camp for his contributions to the amateur game and George Halas for his efforts at the professional level.

Walter Camp: Father of American Football

He was born the son of a school headmaster. Slender to the point of being skinny, it was his desire to excel rather than his physical prowess that caused him to become one of the outstanding sports figures.

He was a pitcher in baseball, a back in Football, a swimmer, a track star. In all these disciplines Walter Camp was the best as he represented Yale in the late 1800s.

Although an outstanding player and coach at Yale University, where he introduced the idea of guards running interference and the centre snap to the punter, Walter Camp's greatest contributions came through his service on the Rules Committee. He became a member in 1887, while still playing for Yale, and served as chairman for over forty years.

Camp, more than anyone else, formulated the rules which changed Football from Rugby into the game as it is played today. Perhaps the greatest change was the rule requiring a team to make five yards in three downs or surrender the ball. Prior to the adoption of this rule the ball was placed in a neutral zone and both teams made a brutal charge for possession. He constantly pressed for rules which would make the game safer for the players and more of a pleasure to watch.

The first All-American squad was the Walter Camp All-American Team. He was so respected in the American Football community that selection by him was the highest distinction any American Football player could aspire to!

Walter Camp's title 'The father of American Football' is undisputed. Ironically, he died in 1925 while attending a meeting of the Rules Committee.

George Halas: godfather of American Football

Other coaching greats made outstanding contributions to the collegiate game, but George Halas is without a doubt the godfather of the professional game.

Halas played under Bob Zuppke at the University of Illinois and during naval service in World War I he starred on the Great Lakes Naval Training Station team. That squad played and won in the Rose Bowl.

After the war he worked for a factory in Decatur, Illinois, where he was also a member of the factory football team. In 1920, Halas organized a meeting which led to the foundation of the National Football League. This meeting brought together representatives of industrial teams in the area, and out of it a twelve team league was formed.

In 1921, Halas moved his team to Chicago. He was now player, coach and owner of the 'Chicago Bears'. The league in which the Bears played became officially known as the National Football League in 1923 and by 1925 it was attracting big collegiate stars. Red Grange, an immortal of American Football history, signed to play with the Bears that year.

Halas owned the Bears for sixty-three years and actually coached them for forty. During his coaching tenure, they won eight NFL titles. It seems fitting that the 1986 world championship team was coached by Mike Ditka, one of 'Papa Bear's' former players.

Opposite above: *Walter Camp*
Princeton plays Yale in an 1879 game of Rugby-type football

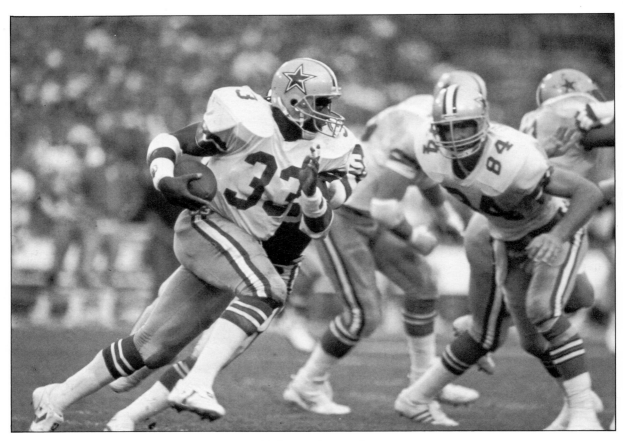

Dallas on the attack

2 Development of the pro game

The fun-loving, hard-hitting young men from the universities were first tempted to 'play for pay' in 1892. The records in the Professional Hall of Fame reflect that a certain Pudge Heffelfinger of Yale got $500 to play in a game in Pittsburgh, Pennsylvania. Indeed, the State of Pennsylvania is called the Home of Professional Football and that is right and fair.

Unfortunately, the next 'pro' only got $20 and by 1906 professional Football had its first scandal. Two teams in Ohio, the Massillon Tigers and the Canton Bulldogs, met. The underdog team, the Tigers, brought off a surprising victory, debarking the Bulldogs 12–6. The Bulldog coach, Blondy Wallace, had bribed one of his players to 'throw' the game so he could win on bets he had placed against his own team. The scandal ruined Football in Canton and set back the advance of the professional game for several years.

It was to be almost a decade later that pro Football got a new start. In the 1912 Olympics, Jim Thorpe won both the decathlon and the pentathlon, causing King Gustav of Sweden to remark, 'You, sir, are the greatest athlete in the world.' In 1920 the American Football League was formed and Jim Thorpe was elected president. There were eleven teams from just four states:

Canton, Ohio
Cleveland, Ohio
Dayton, Ohio
Akron, Ohio
Massillon, Ohio
Rochester, New York
Hammond, Indiana
Muncie, Indiana
Chicago, Illinois
Rock Island, Illinois
Decatur, Illinois

At the end of the first disorganized season, three teams claimed the championship. Massillon quit the league in disgust. George Halas took his Decatur team to Chicago and called them the Bears. Next season Green Bay, Wisconsin, entered a team in the league. So by 1921, the new 'National Football League' was gaining popularity and the game was on its way. Almost every city had a team of stature. Some of the great professionals turned out for these semi-pro teams. One of the finest quarterbacks the game has known, Johnny Unitas, emerged from the 'sand lot' competition. The term 'sand lot' is still used today. It means that the playing field was whatever was available. Many a time the pasture would simply have a patch mowed to form a rudimentary football field. It wasn't unusual to have a short delay in the game when a tackled player slid where a cow had been earlier in the day. Usually the field had no maintenance and any grass soon disappeared, leaving bare sand.

The Green Bay Packers are the only outfit to come from a small city and continuously field a team from 1920 until the present. The city has a population that is smaller than the seating capacity of the stadium, yet there is a great deal of truth in the saying that the only way to get a season ticket to a Packers' game is to inherit it. It doesn't matter what the record was the past season, or how many years it has been since they had a winning season. When the leaves begin to change colour and Football is in the air, everybody in Green Bay is convinced they'll have a winner. 'The Pack is back'.

By 1926 the NFL was settling into a ten-team league, with an Eastern Division and a Western Division. In 1936 it held its first 'draft' of the college (i.e., university) players. This was one of the best things to happen to the sport because a very fair system was devised, whereby the team with the worst record got the first choice of new college stars, the second worst team got the second, and so on. Thus a rich team couldn't buy the best new blood each season and dominate the league. This gave new hope for better fortunes in the future if a team was down.

The War followed and the game took its rightful back seat to the bigger event. In 1945 a new league was formed and it competed for the same spectators. It was called the All-American Football Conference (AA). Keep in mind that there were still many cities with the semi-pro teams. In 1952 one of your authors was moving the yard markers in a game between the Green Bay Packers and the Chippewa Falls Marines!

By 1949 the two rival leagues merged, but it was really the end of all teams in the AA league with the exception of Cleveland, Baltimore and San Francisco. The rest were swallowed up in the NFL, or fell by the wayside. Pete Rozelle took over as Commissioner of the NFL in 1959. There were twelve teams then and they were playing in front of about three million paying customers. That number was about the same as the number of television gridiron spectators in Britain in 1986. In 1941 the Los Angeles franchise had sold for $100,000. In 1963 it changed hands at $7,100,000. Pay for play was big business and getting bigger.

A new 'American Football League' was organized in 1960 with teams in Buffalo, Boston, Houston, Dallas, Los Angeles, Oakland, Denver and New York. They fared so-so in terms of money and attendance. Then in 1964 they signed an Alabama quarterback by the name of Joe Namath for the unheard-of terms of $400,000 for three years. This started a bidding war between the two leagues. Players were signing for sums that exceeded the total team salary of ten years before. The two leagues were bidding themselves into bankruptcy.

On 5 June, 1966 the two leagues announced that they were going to merge. The champions of the two leagues met in 1967. It was to be the game of all games, the 'world championship' (despite the fact that Americans were only playing themselves). It was called the 'Super Bowl'. Green Bay of the NFL beat Kansas City of the AFL on that historic occasion by a score of 35–10.

The following year, the NFL play-off game was held in Green Bay to decide which NFL squad should go to the Super Bowl. The temperature was just right for polar bears. There was a 15 m.p.h. howling wind, with a 'chill factor' equivalent to 49 degrees below zero. That day was to popularize the quote, 'Green Bay might not be the end of the world, but you can see it from there.'

The Dallas Cowboys were leading by a score of 17–14. Green Bay had the ball on the one-yard line, there were 16 seconds left in the game. Bart Starr, quarterback, called time out and conferred with his coach, Vince Lombardi. They could take the sure field goal for three points and tie the game. As Bart Starr was to say later, 'A tie is like kissing your sister.' He carried the ball into the end zone for the touchdown and the right to represent the NFL in the second Super Bowl, where Green Bay beat Oakland 33–14.

The NFL was seen as a much stronger conference than the AFL and the two Super Bowls seemed to prove the point. Going into number three, the brash quarterback of the New York Jets (AFL) guaranteed a win over the Baltimore Colts (NFL), despite the fact that the Jets were clear 18-point underdogs. 'Broadway' Joe Namath, who had cost all that money in 1964, true to his word, connected on 17 of 28 passes for a total of 206 yards leading the Jets to the most stunning upset in pro Football history, 16–7.

The following year, television contracts were straightened out between the two conferences and they merged into the arrangement that we view today. For the past couple of years *another* new league, the USFL, has been trying to expand into the world of pro Football but its future is uncertain.

The student of American Football must remember that teams changed locations and identity for the simple reason that they were professional teams and their primary purpose was to make a profit. But from 1967 onwards, for reasons of order and clarity, the NFL has divided the teams into conferences and within these conferences, divisions. Tradition, location and history played a part in deciding which team would be in which conference

'Football doesn't build character, it eliminates the weak ones.'

DARRELL ROYAL,
UNIVERSITY OF TEXAS

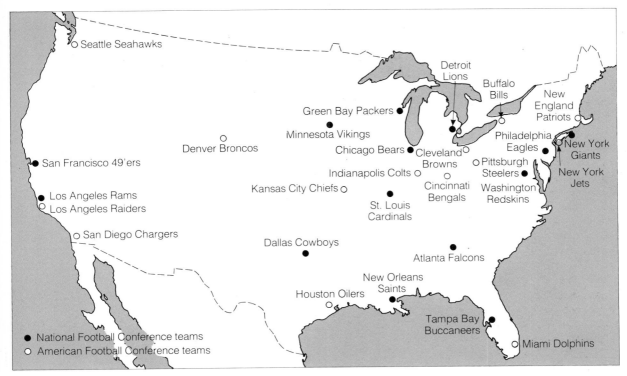

Seattle Seahawks ○

Detroit Lions

Buffalo Bills

New England Patriots ○

Green Bay Packers ●

Denver Broncos ○

Minnesota Vikings ●

Chicago Bears ●

Cleveland Browns ○

Philadelphia Eagles ○

New York Giants ●

Pittsburgh Steelers ○

San Francisco 49'ers ●

Indianapolis Colts ○

Cincinnati Bengals ●

Washington Redskins ●

New York Jets ○

Kansas City Chiefs ○

St. Louis Cardinals ●

Los Angeles Rams ●
Los Angeles Raiders ○

San Diego Chargers ○

Dallas Cowboys ●

Atlanta Falcons ●

New Orleans Saints ●

Houston Oilers ○

Tampa Bay Buccaneers ●

Miami Dolphins ○

● National Football Conference teams
○ American Football Conference teams

and which division. Once this was established, each team was challenged to win its division, then its conference and then go to the Super Bowl.

American Football Conference

EASTERN DIVISION | COACH (1986)

Miami Dolphins | Don Shula
New England Patriots | Raymond Berry
Buffalo Bills | Kay Stephenson
New York Jets | Joe Walton
Indianapolis Colts | Rod Dowhower

CENTRAL DIVISION

Cincinnati Bengals | Sam Wyche
Cleveland Browns | Marty Schottenheimer
Houston Oilers | Hugh Campbell
Pittsburgh Steelers | Chuck Noll

WESTERN DIVISION

Denver Broncos | Dan Reeves
Kansas City Chiefs | John Mackovic
Los Angeles Raiders | Tom Flores
San Diego Chargers | Don Coryell
Seattle Seahawks | Chuck Knox

National Football Conference

EASTERN DIVISION | COACH (1986)

New York Giants | Bill Parcells
St. Louis Cardinals | Jim Hanifan
Washington Redskins | Joe Gibbs
Dallas Cowboys | Tom Landry
Philadelphia Eagles | Marion Campbell

CENTRAL DIVISION

Chicago Bears | Mike Ditka
Tampa Bay Buccaneers | Leeman Bennett
Green Bay Packers | Forrest Gregg
Detroit Lions | Darryl Rogers
Minnesota Vikings | Bud Grant

WESTERN DIVISION

San Francisco 49'ers | Bill Walsh
Los Angeles Rams | John Robinson
New Orleans Saints | Bum Phillips
Atlanta Falcons | Dan Henning

Super Bowl – the record

The American Football League had challenged the National Football League for years, asking the question, 'which league was ultimately the best?' Everyone knew the answer was the NFL, but the Super Bowl had been set up to symbolically settle the question. For the first two Bowls, as we have seen, the predicted result was correct. Then there was the Big Upset. The record is as follows:

1967 Green Bay 35 Kansas City 10
1968 Green Bay 33 Oakland 14
1969 New York Jets 16 Baltimore 7
1970 Kansas City 23 Minnesota 7
1971 Baltimore 16 Dallas 13
1972 Dallas 24 Miami 3
1973 Miami 14 Washington 7
1974 Miami 24 Minnesota 7
1975 Pittsburgh 16 Minnesota 6
1976 Pittsburgh 21 Dallas 17
1977 Oakland 32 Minnesota 14
1978 Dallas 27 Denver 10
1979 Pittsburgh 35 Dallas 31
1980 Pittsburgh 31 Los Angeles 19
1981 Oakland 27 Philadelphia 10
1982 San Francisco 26 Cincinnati 21
1983 Washington 27 Miami 17
1984 Los Angeles Raiders 38 Washington 9
1985 San Francisco 38 Miami 16
1986 Chicago 38 New England 3

Selection for the Super Bowl

When the regular season ends, the three divisional champions in each of the two conferences (National and American) are involved in a play-off for their conference championship. Since it is easier to have an even number of teams playing off in each conference, a fourth team is also chosen. The two teams in the conference with the fourth and fifth best records play each other to determine who will be that fourth team. These are the 'wild card' entries. The conference champions then meet in the Super Bowl.

Super Bowl Most Valuable Players

In each of the Super Bowl games a player is selected as the person who contributed the most to that game. It is to be expected that the player will be from the winning team, and usually a back field man who has had the opportunity to score touchdowns or a receiver who has had the opportunity to catch passes, some for touchdowns.

The quarterback has the best opportunity to be selected because he handles the ball on each play; for this reason, if things go badly, he can take most of the blame for negative play!

Remember now, this 'MVP' is the best of the best in professional football.

These are the names of MVPs selected from Super Bowl I to Super Bowl XX.

I	Bart Starr	Packers
II	Bart Starr	Packers
III	Joe Namath	Jets
IV	Len Dawson	Chiefs
V	Chuck Howley	Cowboys
VI	Roger Staubach	Cowboys
VII	Jake Scott	Dolphins
VIII	Larry Csonka	Dolphins
IX	Franco Harris	Steelers
X	Lynn Swann	Steelers
XI	Fred Biletnikoff	Raiders
XII	Randy White	
	Harvey Martin	Cowboys
XIII	Terry Bradshaw	Steelers
XIV	Terry Bradshaw	Steelers
XV	Jim Plunkett	Raiders
XVI	Joe Montana	49'ers
XVII	John Riggins	Redskins
XVIII	Marcus Allen	Raiders
XIX	Joe Montana	49'ers
XX	Richard Dent	Bears

Richard Dent

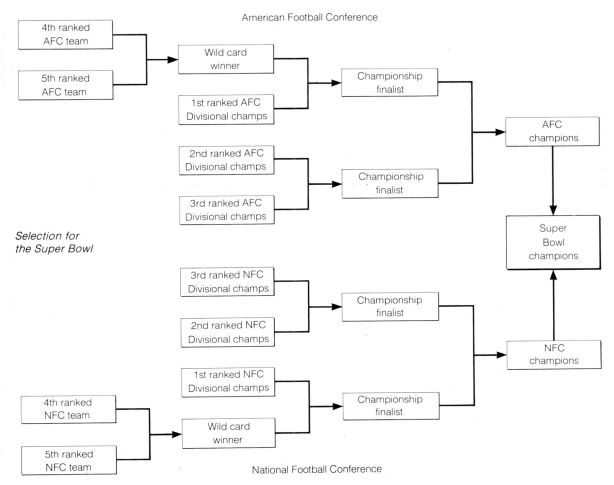

American Football Conference

Selection for
the Super Bowl

National Football Conference

Selection to this Most Valuable role is much more than a matter of ego: the award could be worth over two million dollars in endorsements. The $36,000 they get for the game works out to be about $8,000 per minute of competition. The number of seconds of actual action for the individual player adds up to about four minutes for the game. Legendary Miami running back Larry Csonka put it this way: 'Professional football is the toughest way to earn easy money.' He still bears the scars.

There was an unusual case in 1986. Richard Dent, an eighth-round draft choice in 1983, had the distinction of earning a Chicago Bear salary of $90,000. Good by most standards. Yet, the *average* NFL player was earning just over $200,000 for the season in 1986.

Poor in comparison, Richard Dent was not average. He led the league in sacking (smothering) the quarterback. A 'sack' is tackling the quarterback behind the line of scrimmage for both a loss of yardage and a loss of play. He had 17 for the season. With the Super Bowl game tied at 3–3 he got his first sack. Less than a minute later he got his second sack, causing a fumble. On the next series of downs he put a tackle on Craig James that could be heard in the top row of the stadium. James coughed up the ball; that led to another touchdown and the game was out of reach for the opposing New England Patriots.

When the eleven sports journalists cast their vote for the MVP of Super Bowl XX, the deserving winner was underpaid, under-recognized, but not to be forgotten in the near future. Six feet five inches tall, two hundred and thirty-eight pounds – defensive end Richard Dent was the 'Best of the Best' in Super Bowl XX.

McMahon taking the snap

3 Ball-handling

The whole game of football is about who does what with the ball. You score with it; you can't score without it. How the ball is handled is therefore a very important part of the game.

The basis of the game is that you must make a gain of ten yards in four plays or surrender the ball to your opponent. It is hoped that after making the ten-yard gain a certain number of times you are going to score a touchdown or get close enough to kick a field goal.

The last thing you want to do is turn the ball over to your opponent.

The turnover

Most football games are won or lost by the exchange of ball possession. The team with the ball has the opportunity to score. They can score a touchdown or score by kicking a field goal. If they give away that advantage, the disaster is called a 'turnover'. How does the team give the ball away?

First of all, they don't do it on purpose! It is usually caused by an exceptional reaction by the defense or a mental error on the part of the ball carrier. Most coaches accept that there is only one proper way to carry the football. In the cover photo you will note how it is cradled by the arm. One end is held securely between the elbow socket and chest, while the fingers cover the other end.

If you look at some ball carriers (and this includes many good ones), they will try to cradle the pigskin in their *hand*. This may be more comfortable for running, but the good defensive man will sacrifice part of the force of the tackle, in an attempt to 'strip the ball'. Note in the photo on p. 27, the defensive man is really just trying to get his hand or arm between the ball and the ball carrier's body.

When the ball is raked loose, it becomes a free ball, called a 'fumble'. Usually the defense has the best opportunity to go for the fumbled ball because they are by definition focussing on the offensive advance of it.

To carry the ball properly, tucked in tight, usually slows down the ball carrier. So there is a 'trade off'. They go for maximum speed and then pull the ball in prior to contact. In the third play of Super Bowl XX, Walter Payton went for the extra yard. It was one of his few fumbles.

If we go back and examine this business of ball-handling, there is a lot we can understand about the game. The play starts with the centre 'hiking' the ball (handing it back through his legs). If the quarterback is taking the hike as a direct hand-off, the centre can keep his head up and have a better chance of blocking. This is called 'coming off the ball'. Note the photo opposite. The centre is handing the ball back through his legs with a sharp fast delivery, all the while being able to look at the defense and prepare for his blocking assignment.

Now, if the ball is passed back to a kicker or the quarterback in a short punt position, the centre must 'at least sneak a peek', to see where he is delivering the ball. This means, for that micro-second that he is looking through his legs, he is at the mercy of any defensive move in front of him.

The basic rule of thumb, so far as blame for turnovers goes, is that the centre is responsible for getting the ball to the quarterback. After that, it is the responsibility of the quarterback to get the ball to the back, or in the air to a pass receiver.

The back then has the responsibility of taking care of the ball as he tries to gain the maximum amount of yardage. We have to acknowledge that the back might be getting the ball from somebody other than the quarterback. It might be a punt

return. It might be a kick-off. It might be a field goal attempt or it might be a pass interception.

In taking a punt or kick-off the back usually tries for a running start. He wants some forward motion when he gets the ball. However, if the ball is high and the kicking team is there, he will choose to go for the 'fair catch'. By raising one hand straight above his head he signals to the other players and officials that he is going to catch the ball but not advance it. He is then allowed to do this unhindered.

If after signalling a 'fair catch' he does advance the ball, he is penalized. If he is hit by the kicking team after signalling the fair catch, *they* are penalized. This often leads to disputes. You can imagine, as that ball is dropping out of the sky, everybody wants to make a decision at the last second.

The pass interception is another example of 'ball exchange'. You again need to envision the complexity and courage of conviction in the receiver going for the pass, The defensive man is usually moving toward the ball. This means that the receiver has to concentrate on catching the ball knowing that the defensive man is going to 'blast' him. It is no wonder that at the school level the term 'hearing footsteps' is used. Some inexperienced receivers devote more concern to the defensive tackle than to the ball, though this seldom happens at the professional level.

It must also be appreciated that, for the most part, the offense and defense are going for the ball from opposite directions. If the airborne pigskin goes over the defensive man and is caught, it can go all the way for a touchdown. For the defensive man to move in and cut it off, he has to be moving in the opposite direction of the play flow. If he intercepts, there could well be a touchdown for the defense, since there may be nobody in a position to stop his momentum.

It was Frank Smouse who said, 'What's tough about pass defense is that there is only one ball.' Which means that the defense can do practically everything right and *still* get caught out on the one move that matters.

Opposite above: *Broken tackle. He will go for yards*

Opposite below: *Hearing footsteps*

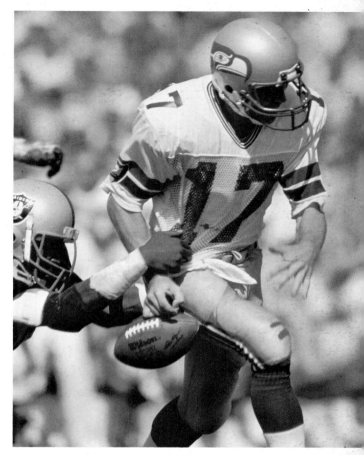

Stripping the ball

In coaching, playing and watching football it is always interesting to observe what we call 'ball attitude'. There truly are some players who think the ball belongs to them. As a player or coach you notice players that have this 'ball attitude'. Every time it pops free as if by magic they are there to claim it. The records kept in schools or on the pro teams always identify the person who gains that loose ball, be it a fumble or pass interception. The possessive player is remembered.

Most coaches regard a turnover as worth two points, recognizing that one out of three times you should expect to advance the ball and score the six point touchdown. With the field goal range getting longer through improved kicking techniques and the evolution of the shape of the football, the turnover might be getting even more important.

4 The basics

The ball

The ball itself has undergone many changes, beginning as round and developing into a prolate spheroid shape. The present dimensions are:

length, between 11 and $11\frac{1}{4}$ inches,

short circumference, from $21\frac{1}{4}$ to $21\frac{1}{2}$ inches,

long circumference, from 28 to $28\frac{1}{2}$ inches.

As the passing game increased in popularity, the ball became longer and slimmer to accommodate bullet-like passing. This streamlined shape had a negative effect on kicking. Despite the fact that streamlined footballs and improved kicking techniques are making the field goal range longer, the terrific 60-yard field goals common in the days of the more oval ball are now seldom seen.

The ball has a slit in one seam where the rubber bladder has been inserted. This slit is closed with laces, which provide grip on the ball. Most quarterbacks prefer the laces at their fingertips so that the ball rolls off the fingers on a pass with the lace being the last point of contact.

The field

The modern football field retains the rectangular shape used in other football games over the past 2000 years. The dimensions have changed many times and the present measurements were established in 1912.

The field is 120 yards long and $53\frac{1}{3}$ yards wide. It is divided by parallel lines every five yards for 100 yards. Ten yards in from each end there is a goal line, making the actual playing area 100 yards long. The two additional ten yard areas are called end zones. Passes, punts, and kick-offs may be handled in the end zones, but scoring takes place at the goal line. A field is diagrammed on the following page.

Note that in high school and college the 'inbound' lines are 53 feet 4 inches from the side-

Opposite: *Houston Astrodome inside and out*

The all-time great put down

The football may be said to have narrowed some people's horizons. See what you think of this. In 1982 a group of American Football coaches were enjoying a steak dinner and the amenities on the shore of the Marmara Sea in Turkey.

One football story led to another and finally one of the wives had heard enough. She said, 'Look, if you are all university graduates and experienced educators, you should be able to talk about something more important than football.'

With that she addressed Gary Flannery at the far end of the table. Gary was the football coach at one of the American high schools in Turkey. 'Gary, let's discuss something philosophical. Evil. Let's discuss Evil.'

There was a pause.

'Gary, what do you think of evil?'

He looked her straight in the eye and said, 'I think he is going to kill himself if he doesn't quit riding those motorcycles!'

'I thought I had a lifetime contract. Then I found out that if I had a losing season they were going to declare me legally dead.'

HEYDEN FRY
COACH, UNIVERSITY OF IOWA

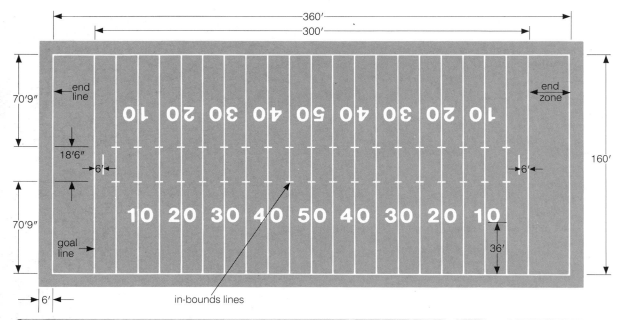

- 360'
- 300'
- 70'6" — end line
- 18'6"
- 6'
- 70'9" — goal line
- 160'
- end zone
- 6'
- 36'

10 20 30 40 50 40 30 20 10
10 20 30 40 50 40 30 20 10

in-bounds lines

The field

lines. The in-bounds lines are simply where the ball is placed after it has gone out of bounds to recommence play. The pro teams want it more to the centre of the playing area than is desired in college. If the ball is positioned for the start of the play closer to one side of the field than the other, it provides more opportunities for different types of running plays. If it is close to the centre of the field at the start of the play, there is better balance for passing. This is the reason for the different location of in-bounds lines.

Of course, in Rugby, the ball starts from the side of the field where it went out of bounds.

The American Football field is usually surrounded with a seating arrangement for spectators. This seating capacity might vary from a couple of hundred seats in a high school game to 107,000 at the University of Southern California. By having an individual seat for each spectator the problems of crowd control are greatly reduced. This is important when viewing a game as violent and emotional as American Football.

In the pros there is a variety of stadiums to host the spectators. Over the past years and especially after the 1967 play-off game in Green Bay, Wisconsin, which was marred by the weather, teams have tried for covered stadiums. One of the best of these 'domes' is the Superdome in New Orleans.

It was built at a cost of $165 million. Seating almost 100,000 people, the steel roof that spans it covers an area of 9·7 acres. There are almost 400 miles of electrical wiring with some 15,000 outlets and lights, all computerized. The underground parking holds 5000 cars and 250 buses. It opened in 1975 and the events it houses, which apart from football include rock concerts and other crowd-pullers, have netted the state of Louisiana some $2,678 million in profits. It was a good investment.

Of course the Superdome has artificial turf, no wind factor, constant temperature and in the opinion of some of the 'old timers' it might just detract from the raw elements of the game. Still, the football field has come a long way from the days of cutting the grass on part of a farmer's field.

Goal posts

The goal posts are located at each end of the field and in the middle of the goal lines. The posts are in the perpendicular plane of the goal line. The

Field goal attempt

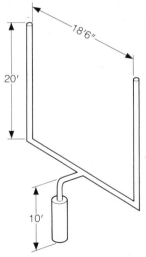

crossbar is 18 feet 6 inches wide and its top surface is 10 feet above the playing field. The vertical uprights extend from each end of the crossbar to a height of 20 feet or more.

The scoring zone is the plane above the crossbar to any height, but within the projection of the vertical uprights.

The Poe football family

Edgar Allen Poe had six great-nephews and they were as well-versed in Football as he was in the world of letters. Two of them made All-American, Edgar Allen in 1889 and Arthur in 1899.

The folks at Yale University still talk about the time they were leading with seven seconds to go. Arthur, who had never kicked a field goal in a game and was playing with a broken nose, drilled the ball between the uprights as the gun sounded.

All the Yale fans could think was, 'Thank goodness that Arthur was the last of the Poes.' He graduated that spring, so they could say with the Raven, 'Nevermore!'

Knute Rockne

From 1910 until his untimely death in a plane crash in 1930, Notre Dame University was the centre of Knute Rockne's existence. He was a star player at Notre Dame for three years, assistant coach for three more and head coach from 1918 until 1930.

His emphasis on fundamentals and drill produced teams famous for their timing, speed and flawless execution. He is also remembered as a master psychologist.

One of his most quoted lines, 'Let's win one for the Gipper,' refers to George Gipp, a fine triple-threat back, who died of pneumonia during the season of 1920. A movie based on the life of Rockne was produced in the 1930s, and an obscure young actor named Ronald Reagan was cast as the 'Gipper'.

Rockne was one of the earliest exponents of the forward pass and also anticipated the modern platoon system. His practice of starting a game with a team of shock troops whose purpose was to wear down the opponents before sending in the first team was certainly a forerunner of today's specialist squads.

Running back preparing to lateral

JOHN RALSTON

former Denver Broncos coach, explaining his departure from the team:

'I left because of illness and fatigue. The fans were sick and tired of me.'

'We didn't lose, we just ran out of time.'
VINCE LOMBARDI
GREEN BAY PACKERS COACH

5 Timing, equipment and scoring

Timing

The official game time is sixty minutes of actual clocked play. Of course this is greatly extended by various intervals and stoppages. The sixty minutes are preceded by a flip of a coin with the winning captain having his choice of kicking, receiving, or which end of the field to defend. Should he choose to receive the kick-off, the losing captain has the choice of goal lines to defend. Wind direction and velocity play an important part in this choice. At the beginning of the second half the loser of the coin-toss has first choice.

The game is divided into four quarters of fifteen minutes each. At the end of the first quarter the teams change ends. Following the second quarter there is a fifteen-minute half-time interval, and ends are again changed after the third quarter.

Each team is allowed three time-outs of $1\frac{1}{2}$ minutes duration in each half.

Under professional rules, draws may be broken by adding one or more sudden death overtime periods.

The official clock is stopped in the following situations:

a. end of a period
b. when a foul is committed
c. when a fair catch is caught
d. when a score occurs
e. when a player is injured
f. when equipment repair is needed
g. when the ball goes out of bounds
h. when teams change possession of the ball
i. when the 'two minutes remaining' signal is given.

At the end of a play, when all the dust has settled, the official will signal that a second clock has started. This second clock is set for twenty-five seconds at the school and university levels and at thirty seconds for the professionals. Its purpose is to prevent time-wasting between plays. The offensive team must put the ball back in play prior to the end of that twenty-five or thirty second-period. Failure to do so means a penalty of five yards.

PEPPER ROGERS

former Georgia Tech football coach, noting that he got fired the day after he had lunch with President Jimmy Carter:

'I'm the only coach in history to go straight from the White House to the outhouse.'

Equipment

No equipment was worn in the very first game, between Rutgers and Princeton in 1869, but as the rules changed and more direct contact was made, protective equipment developed.

Today each player must wear the basic protective gear.

Helmet (with facemask): The helmet is made of hard plastic and lined with suspended cushions. Usually the cushions contain airbags and can be adjusted to the player's head size.

Shoulder pads: These are made of plastic with soft padding underneath. Suspensions under the plastic rest on the shoulder next to the neck. This directs the force down the middle of the body and away from the point of the shoulder.

Hip pads: These vary considerably. They all protect the hip bones on the sides and the kidneys and tailbone in the back.

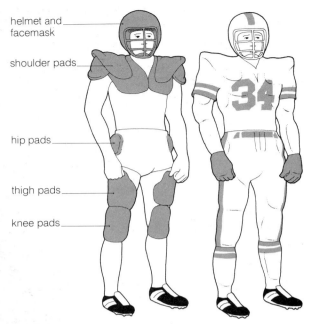

helmet and facemask

shoulder pads

hip pads

thigh pads

knee pads

Thigh pads: These have a soft surface covering a hard pad and are worn to protect the thigh muscles from sharp blows.

Knee pads: These are soft pads usually held in pockets within the pants.

Extra equipment

Some players wear additional equipment such as rib pads, shin pads, forearm pads, elbow pads and gloves.

In high school and university, all players must wear a rubber or soft plastic mouth piece. While it protects the teeth, the main purpose is to prevent a blow from the chin being transferred through vibration to the brain.

Is all the armour necessary? This question is often asked and most players would say 'yes'.

> The facemask was added to the helmet around 1950. Many of the retired players can easily be identified as having played their football pre-facemask.
>
> Bob Vansuch, a player from Campbell, Ohio, was asked if it was true that he had broken his nose eight times. He replied, 'No! I didn't. Eight other guys did.'

Uniforms

The uniform consists of pants and jersey. Usually a team will have two sets, with their team colours switched around a white jersey or coloured jersey, depending on whether they are playing home or away. When two teams meet, one can then be in a light colour and the other dark.

Numbers must be worn on both the front and the back of the jersey. This helps the officials (and spectators) to identify players involved in infractions of the rules. It also enables the spectators to follow their favourite players.

The offensive positions have numbers assigned as follows (there are no strict rules for defensive numbers):

quarterbacks	1–19
running backs	20–49
centres	50–59
guards	60–69
tackles	70–79
ends	80–89

> MIKE DITKA
>
> on his reputation for meanness when he was a defensive end:
>
> 'I'm not mean at all. I just try to protect myself. And you'll see I don't ever pick on anybody who has a number above 50.'

Helmets at the helm

President Lyndon B. Johnson, commenting on Gerald R. Ford, former centre for the University of Michigan and himself later President:

'The trouble with Ford is that he played too many years of football without a helmet.'

A few years later, when Ford was campaigning in the presidential primaries against Ronald Reagan, the latter was asked if he had played college football.

'Yes,' he replied, 'but when I played, *I* wore a helmet.'

Scoring

There are four ways a team can score in football. They are the touchdown, the field goal, the try-for-point or 'point after touchdown', and the safety.

However, prior to scoring, in almost all instances, success in football depends on ball possession. Each time you have the ball, you must gain ten yards within four tries or plays. If you don't gain the ten yards, you must surrender the ball to your opponents.

Thus, 'first and ten' (first down and ten yards to gain) is always recognized as the key to most scoring opportunities. The offensive strategy depends on gaining that yardage and the next 'first down', retaining possession of the ball and the opportunity to score.

Touchdown: A touchdown (6 points) is scored when a player crosses the opponents' goal line with the ball or gains possession of the ball in the opponents' end zone. (See colour picture.)

Field goal: A field goal (3 points) is scored by placing the ball on the ground and kicking it through the goal posts, above the crossbar.

Point after (or try-for-point): This is the conversion opportunity given the team after they score a touchdown. The ball is placed on the two-yard line, and the team has one play to kick for the single point in the style of a field goal.

Safety: The defensive team may score a two-point safety by stopping the team with the ball in their own end zone. The team the safety is scored *against* must kick-off to the other team from the twenty-yard line.

Scores with differing values lead to game strategy. For example, a team leading by six points with 45 seconds remaining on the clock might deliberately ground the ball in their own end zone rather than risk a blocked punt. This would result in a safety and two points against them, but they would still have a four-point lead and be allowed a free kick from their own twenty-yard line.

After receiving the kick well downfield the opponents would have only 45 seconds in which to score a touchdown. It would not do them any good

Celebrating the score

to get within field-goal range and go for the kick. The field goal is three points and would still leave them in a losing position. The odds are against the touchdown. So even scoring against yourself, under some conditions, could allow you to win the game!

Up and over (rather than up and under) on the wedge

6 The rules

There are three basic sets of football rules used in the United States. The rules vary to meet the needs of high school, collegiate, and professional football.

High school teams are governed by the National Federation of State High School Associations, most commonly called 'Federation Rules'. However, some high school conferences prefer to use college rules.

College teams are governed by the National Collegiate Athletic Association (NCAA), usually called the 'NC double A'.

The American Professional Football Association, established in 1920, has evolved into the National Football League, and its rules govern professional football.

Each year there are minor changes in the rules. The two basic reasons for changes are to reduce injuries and to make the game more enjoyable for spectators.

Television, through instant replay, has contributed to a clearer understanding of rules, rule interpretation, violations, and penalties.

Following the 1950 introduction of helmets with facemasks, the next and most serious concern in rule changes had to do with protecting the knees. Knee injuries continue to be a major worry even though the present rules have made great strides in reducing the injuries.

Many ex-players have knees that look as though they lost a duel with a midget swordsman. Those who bear the scars from twenty years ago are reminded on cold and wet days of a 'crackback block', or a defensive tackle 'piling on' at the end of a play. The authors did not escape without torn cartilage, broken ribs, lost teeth, broken noses, broken collar bones, broken fingers, toes and arms.

Rule violations and penalties

The officials are on the field to ensure that all players follow the rules or are penalized for infractions.

The rules, as well as varying between high school, college and the pros, also vary from year to year, but below are the current basic rules used in professional football:

VIOLATION	PENALTY
Piling on	Fifteen yards plus automatic first down
Roughing the kicker	Fifteen yards plus automatic first down
Roughing the passer	Fifteen yards plus automatic first down
Kicking, batting or pushing a loose ball	Fifteen yards
Spearing, butting or ramming an opponent with the helmet	Fifteen yards
Clipping	Fifteen yards
Delay of game (at the start of half)	Fifteen yards
Pass interference	Fifteen yards
Illegal blocking below the waist	Fifteen yards
Illegal crackback block	Fifteen yards
Intentionally grasping opponent's facemask	Fifteen yards
Unnecessary roughness	Fifteen yards
Unsportsmanlike conduct	Fifteen yards
Assisting the runner	Ten yards
Illegal use of hands on offense	Ten yards
Ineligible player downfield on a pass play	Ten yards
Offensive pass interference	Ten yards
Tripping	Ten yards
Defensive holding	Five yards plus automatic first down
Running into the kicker	Five yards plus automatic first down
Illegal use of hands on defense	Five yards plus automatic first down
Throwing a pass from beyond the scrimmage line	Five yards plus loss of down
Crawling	Five yards
Encroachment	Five yards
Excessive time-outs	Five yards
Failure to pause one second following shift or huddle	Five yards
False start	Five yards
Unintentionally grasping opponent's facemask	Five yards

VIOLATION	PENALTY
Illegal formation	Five yards
Illegal motion	Five yards
Illegal return of punt	Five yards
Illegal shift	Five yards
Illegal substitution	Five yards
Ineligible player releasing early on a punt	Five yards
Invalid fair catch signal	Five yards
Kick-off out of bounds	Five yards
Less than seven players on offensive line at the snap	Five yards
More than eleven players on the field	Five yards
More than one man in motion at the snap	Five yards
Offside	Five yards
Player out of bounds at the snap	Five yards
Forward pass out of bounds	Loss of down
Forward pass incomplete or strikes goal posts	Loss of down
Forward pass thrown after ball has passed the line of scrimmage	Loss of down
Forward pass touches ineligible receiver	Loss of down
Second forward pass from behind the line of scrimmage	Loss of down

Scrambling

'During the week I practise law. On Sunday, I am the law.'
TOMMY BELL,
ATTORNEY AND NFL OFFICIAL

7 Officials

If you are new to the game, you can learn a tremendous amount simply by watching the officials ruling on each play. This will give you an insight into how the game works, and the method behind the apparent madness of the action. The officials keep this highly emotional contact game under control. On some calls it is necessary for the referee to get two or more officials together and reach a group decision. All judgment calls are final, even if they are wrong; however, an incorrect rule interpretation, mistake on the number of time-outs, or similar error may be corrected after a challenge by either coach.

The officials indicate that a foul has occurred and a penalty will be considered by tossing a yellow silk flag to the ground at the point of the infraction. If the ball is in play, the whistle is not blown.

High schools use four or five officials, but colleges and professionals have a team of seven on the field, plus the three-man 'chain gang', who measure downs with a chain distance marker, on the sidelines.

The diagram indicates the general position of the seven officials relative to the teams and the chain gang. The key to the diagram (opposite) is as follows:

1. *Referee:* in charge of the team of officials. He gives the captain of a team the options on a penalty and indicates when the clock is running. He lines up behind the offensive team and follows the play. The referee always indicates the call. If another official makes the call, he then goes to the referee, explains the details, and the referee takes over.

2. *Umpire:* lines up in the middle of the defensive backfield. His responsibility is to watch for holding and other violations by interior linemen. He records time-outs.

3. *Head linesman:* positioned on the line of scrimmage, watches for offsides and covers plays coming to his side of the field. He has play-by-play responsibility for the chain gang, their marking of the ball, and the ten-yard measure.

4. *Line judge:* positioned on the scrimmage line, he watches for offsides as well as encroachments. He covers plays that come to his side of the field. He is responsible for the timing of the game and fires the pistol to signal the end of each quarter.

5. *Back judge:* lines up on the same side of the field as the line judge. He is deep in the defense and is responsible for covering long passes on that side of the field.

He assists the field judge in deciding if field goal attempts are good.

6. *Field judge:* lines up deep in the defense and also assists with pass coverage. Usually he is responsible for covering the catching of punts from the line of scrimmage.

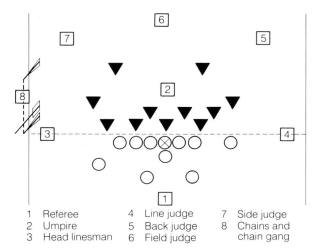

1	Referee	4	Line judge	7	Side judge
2	Umpire	5	Back judge	8	Chains and
3	Head linesman	6	Field judge		chain gang

7. *Side Judge:* lines up on the same side of the field as the head linesman. Checks the wide receiver and back on his side.

8. *The chain gang:* consists of three men. They are responsible for establishing whether or not the ten yards required of the offense has been made.

When the offensive team takes over the ball, they must make ten yards in four or less attempts (plays). So the referee will place the ball on the field, then one of the chain gang will place a stake on the sidelines exactly parallel to the front point of the ball. The second man will pull his stake upfield to where the chain is stretched to its full length of ten yards. The third man has a stake with indicators 1, 2, 3 and 4. They tell what down it is; in other words how many plays have been used. As the ball is advanced by the offensive team, the man with the 'down marker' places his stake parallel to the front point of the ball.

Above: *Official in action*

Opposite: *The chain gang*

The chain gang never goes on the field unless there is a very close call. If the offense is stopped so that the ball is almost parallel to the front stake, the referee will call a time-out. Then he will assist the gang in bringing the chain onto the the field and measuring the front stake against the front of the ball.

This is an exciting moment in a game, especially if it is 4th down. If the ball is not up to the front stake, that means the offense did not make the required ten yards and must relinquish the ball to their opponents.

The referee will be the one to signal to the coaches, players and spectators every time there is a penalty or condition that affects the state of the game.

The following are examples of the most basic signals and the reasons for them.

Time-out

The official running clock is stopped. There are sixty minutes of running time in the game and there are many reasons for stoppages as we have seen (page 35). The officials may have to unpile a crowd of players to find the ball, for example. When time is running short at the end of a game, the team ahead in score will try to keep the clock running, while the team behind will try to stop the clock.

Blocking below the waist

On an open field play such as a punt return or a kick-off return, the blockers are not allowed to execute their blocks below the waist. This is an example of a rule change that is designed to protect the knees of the players.

Illegal cut or blocking below the waist

Clipping

A clip is a block to the backside of an opponent. It is exceptionally dangerous and something that the officials are correct in emphasizing. Many a Football career has been ended by a 'clip'.

Clipping (personal foul)

Dead ball

This signals that the action has stopped and the clock is not running. Once the signal is given, the players have thirty seconds before play is restarted. With the centring of the ball the game is live once again.

Dead ball

First and ten

When the offensive team has gained ten yards in four or less downs, they have a new opportunity. They have a first down and a new ten yards to go.

This is also true when there is an exchange of the ball following a score, punt, or fumble.

First down

An unintentional clip

Holding

It is illegal to grab an opponent to gain an advantage, but the defense may lay hold on a blocker to 'toss' him to the side. However the defensive player may not 'grab, hold and detain'. The *offensive* player never has the right to grab for any reason.

Holding

Illegal procedure or formation

If the offensive team has two men in the backfield moving at the same time, or a back is moving toward the line of scrimmage when the ball is hiked, the procedure is illegal. The offense must also have seven men on the line of scrimmage at the start of the play, or it is an illegal procedure.

Illegal formation or procedure

Interference with a catch

Once the ball has left the passer's hand, both the offense and defense have an equal opportunity to catch it. But neither can interfere with the other. If both are 'going for the ball' and there is incidental contact, that's fair. But if one player tries to gain an unfair advantage, such as holding his hands in front of the eyes of the other man, this is a penalty.

This is one of the most difficult calls in football. The officials must be in perfect position and make that decision in a micro-second. Many professional football players have gone from the game to Hollywood to act in films. Some of us

Interference with a forward pass or fair catch illegal

think their first acting lessons took place on the field, trying to convince an official that they had been interfered with while going for a pass.

Illegal forward pass

A forward pass must be thrown from behind the scrimmage line. Only one forward pass is allowed in any given play. To violate either of these rules is to be penalized for an illegal forward pass.

Illegal forward pass

Invalid fair catch signal

When a defensive player is receiving a punt and the tacklers are close, as we have already seen, he may raise his hand directly above his head, thus signalling that he is going to take a 'fair catch'. This means that the tackles cannot touch him, also that he can't advance the ball.

If he gives a half-way signal so that he can take advantage of the situation, it is invalid and a penalty.

Invalid fair catch signal

Intentionally grounding a pass

Sometimes the passer cannot find an open receiver. If he is about to be tackled, he might toss the ball into the ground. This means there is no chance that he will complete the pass and also that the defense can't get to the ball. Sometimes he craftily tosses it to an open part of the field, to avoid being tackled for a loss in yardage. That incurs a penalty.

Intentional grounding of a pass

Ineligible receiver

The quarterback may send any of the four backfield men or the two ends out for a pass. The centre, the two guards and the two tackles may not go down field. If they do it is an 'ineligible receiver downfield' penalty. One of the reasons for having a numbering system on the jerseys is so that the officials can quickly spot this kind of violation.

The same signal may be given on a punt. The opposing team cannot go after the punt returner until the ball is kicked. The kicking team may not go downfield, either, until the ball is kicked.

Ineligible receiver or ineligible member of kicking team downfield

Out of bounds reception

In the pros, a pass receiver must have both feet in-bounds while catching a pass. In school and university only one foot in-bounds is required. Another difficult call for the officials. The receiver must have the ball under control before leaving the field on a pass that pulls him off the sidelines or out of the end zone. Especially in the pros, the passes are tossed right at the line, because this reduces the chances of the defense intercepting the ball.

Pass juggled inbounds but caught out of bounds

Personal foul

This covers a multitude of sins. If any player tries to gain an advantage over

another, external to normal procedures, it is a personal foul. An example would be a defensive man, rather than using the forearm to ward off a blocker, projecting an elbow to the jaw.

Tripping

A player may not extend his arms or legs to trip an opponent, except to tackle the man with the ball.

Tripping

Delay of game, excessive time-outs

As already indicated, there are two clocks on the scoreboard. One is the running time, the other measures the time it takes for the offensive team to get the ball in play. They have thirty seconds after the referee signals that the play is set to start. If the quarterback can't select a play, call it, get his team lined up and have the ball centred in that thirty seconds, he has delayed the game.

If a team calls a time-out after they have used all of theirs up, it is a penalty.

If players intentionally move slowly in getting up after a tackle or block to use up time, the officials may call a 'delay of game'.

Delay of game or excess time-out

Offside or encroachment

Prior to putting the ball in play, neither team may go into the neutral zone on the line of scrimmage. If they cross the line they are 'offside'. Now, sometimes the offense will try to draw the defense across the line by faking the start of a play with a slight movement. If they do that, even if a defensive man does cross the line, the penalty is against the offense. It is an encroachment.

Offside or encroaching

Time in, no time-out, start the clock

This signals that the clock is to start running *or* that it should not stop. An example might be when the team behind on the scoreboard tries to run the ball out of bounds, but does not make it. The officials would immediately give this signal to keep the official clock running.

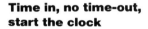

No time-out, or start clock

Safety

The defense can only score by downing the offense with the ball behind their own goal line. That is called a safety and is so indicated.

Score

The offense can score three ways: by the touchdown (worth 6), the point-after-touchdown (worth 1) and the field goal (worth 3). All three, if successful, are indicated by the same signal.

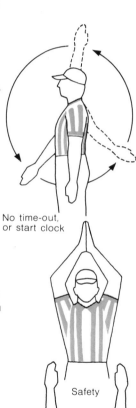

Safety

Player ejected

This should never happen, but sometimes, even the professionals will lose sense of what the game is about and really disadvantage their team. Their services are dispensed with and their team pays with a yardage penalty.

Player ejected

al contact

After a pass receiver is five yards downfield he cannot be touched by the defense. Sometimes, when the receiver is beating the defense to a position, the defense will 'bump' the receiver. That's a penalty.

Illegal contact

Illegal motion

Only one player may be moving in the backfield of the offensive team prior to the start of the play. At the snap of the ball, he must be moving parallel to, or away from, the line of scrimmage. Other motion is going to produce a penalty.

Illegal motion at the snap

Facemask

The facemask was added to the helmet to protect the nose and teeth. It would not make sense to allow another player to use it as a handle and torque the neck. So if it is unintentionally touched it is a five-yard penalty and if deliberately abused, a fifteen-yard penalty.

Grabbing the face mask (personal foul)

Illegal use of hands

Many viewers new to the game think that this has to do with the cheerleaders. Really it is a penalty that can be awarded against either the offense or the defense, though the offense are usually the abusers: they try to extend their blocking areas. The offense may use their hands but they must be employed inside the elbows. It is reaching and grabbing that makes for the violation.

Illegal use of the hands

Helping the ball carrier

It is expected that the ball carrier will follow his blockers and make his own way. Players may not get behind the ball carrier and push or assist. In the 1986 season William Perry tried to pick up his teammate Walter Payton and carry him over the goal-line after he had been stopped. That's a penalty.

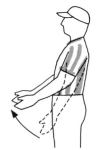

Crawling, pushing, or helping the ballcarrier

Roughing the passer

The quarterback is really 'on the cross' when he releases a pass, and completely vulnerable. His total concentration must be on the receiver. If after the release a defensive man takes a shot at him, it is a necessary penalty. The rules must provide him with this protection.

Running into or roughing the passer (personal foul)

Illegal crackback block

Within the interior of the line, a player can trap, influence, block and get in some cheap shots unseen. But one thing he cannot do any more is to build up a head of steam and come from more than two yards outside the line to wreak havoc on an opposing lineman's legs and knees. This, like the clip, has really produced some limping 'old-timers', with their knees pushed out of their sockets.

Illegal crackbar

Nothing happened

This signal indicates that the spectator has not missed anything if he went out for a beer. If a field goal is no good, a penalty not taken or a pass falls to the ground, this is the signal.

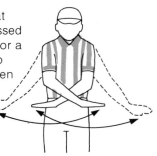

Penalty refused/incomplete pass/play over/missed goal

Loss of down

This signal indicates a loss of down that goes with a penalty or an incomplete pass.

Loss of down

Opposite above: *Official about to make a call*
Opposite below: *The umpire's view of a line play*

'One man practising sportsmanship is far better than a hundred teaching it.'

KNUTE ROCKNE,
COACH, NOTRE DAME

Shutdown! (top)

Your grandmother could ride in her wheelchair through that hole

8 Blocking and tackling

'Football is blocking and tackling. Everything else is mythology.'

VINCE LOMBARDI,
COACH, GREEN BAY PACKERS

Blocking

Blocking, more than anything else, is the key to offensive football. In its simplest form it means getting in the way of a defensive man, or moving the defensive man out of the way of the man with the ball. In reality, it usually ends up being in the simplest form! The execution of a perfect block is almost impossible, for two basic reasons. The blocker is trying to move someone in front of him and at the same time protect a ball carrier behind him. Not being able to see both situations, the blocker must rely on the intended direction of the play and his past experience. While the viewer will witness 'blocks' of every possible configuration, there are really only three basic manoeuvres.

The first is to drive your head straight at the defensive man and slide to the side, putting him on your shoulder, raising and moving him in the opposite direction to the way the ball carrier is going. In our illustration, the blocker will on con-tact snap his head and shoulders upwards to get a lift on the defensive man. If this is accomplished, it is easy to move the man out of the path of the ball carrier.

The second type of block is designed to screen or cross the path of the defensive man. It is called a 'cross-body block'. The blocker throws his body into the defender so that the man with the ball can run by the defensive man using the blocker as a fence or screen.

The third type of block is really just a matter of getting in the face of the rushing defender. It is used for passing, punting and field goals. The blocker simply puts himself in front of the rusher. He hits, gives ground, hits again, gives ground and hopefully by that time the pass, punt, or field goal has been accomplished.

Should the blocker make the mistake of being too aggressive, charging and completely defeating the rushing defensive man, he might 'open a seam' in the pocket and another defensive man might use this seam as a path to the ball.

Blocking has the single purpose of defending the ball carrier.

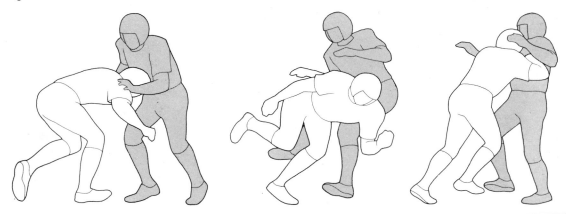

Right: *A gang tackle*

Below: *Nailing him to the ground*

Tackling

With the exception of the 'loose ball' or 'turnover', tackling the ball carrier is the only way the defense can stop the offensive charge.

The reader will appreciate that both the tackler and the ball carrier have an enormous amount of necessary armour. When they meet, each trying to gain an advantage in their respective direction, the collision may impart a force equal to nine G's on each player. That is about the same amount of force that an astronaut experiences escaping the earth's gravitational pull. The defensive man must bring the ball carrier to the ground. The direction in which the ball carrier falls is very important. If he is six feet tall, takes one step forward and then falls forward, he has effectively gained three yards. The reader is reminded that the offense is required to make ten yards in four attempts. It is easy to see that if the ball carrier described were to accomplish the step and forward fall on every play, it would be three yards times four plays – twelve yards. The offense would have a new first and ten situation.

Therefore, tackling requires that the defense attempt to retard the first step and ensure that the ball carrier falls in a direction other than forward. To do this they aim at the 'sweetspot'. The sweetspot is just above the centre of gravity, in the middle of the chest. Good defenders 'nail the man in the ground'. They hit just above the centre of gravity, tip the ball carrier backwards, let his feet fly and then drive him into the deck. If they do it hard enough to divert the ball carrier's attention from the pigskin he is conveying, that's a fumble.

This necessary emphasis on stopping the forward impetus of the ball carrier is a vital element of the game.

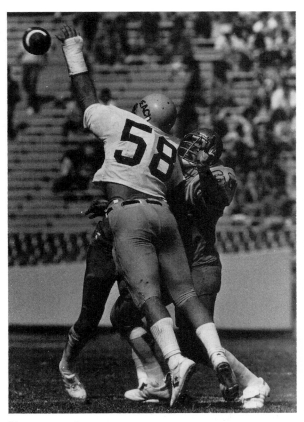

The pass rush

'BIG DADDY' LISCOMB
legendary 288-pound defensive lineman for the Baltimore Colts:

'I just wrap my arms around the whole backfield and peel them off one by one until I get to the ball carrier. Him I keep.'

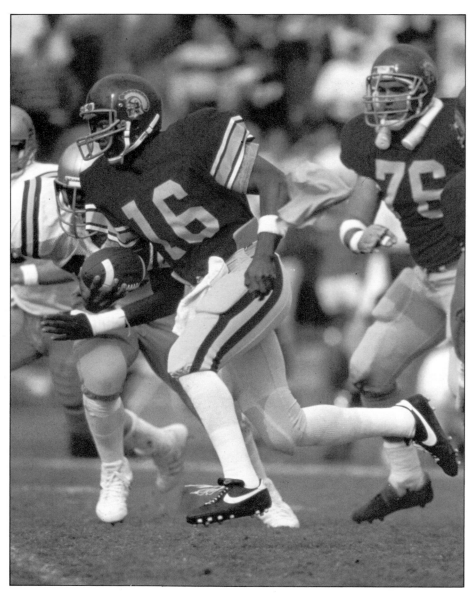

Trojan quarterback Rodney Peete, University of Southern California

9 Offensive football

Early offensive football included formations such as the 'flying wedge'. This primitive formation placed the centre at the point of attack with the rest of the team formed behind him in a V-shaped alignment protecting the ball carrier. On the snap signal the wedge proceeded downfield in bulldozer fashion. Rules were gradually introduced to eliminate such tactics and reduce the advantage of sheer brute force. Football has never completely forsaken force, but deception and speed have become increasingly important aspects of the game.

The rule requiring seven linemen and four backfield men opened up many new approaches to gaining yardage and scoring points.

A brief analysis of various formations provides the reader with a better understanding of football and also leads to the realization that many of today's plays are modifications of much earlier concepts. The following two diagrams (the detailed key is given on the right) serve to illustrate the evolutionary aspects of offensive Football. Note

○	Offensive player
⊗	Offensive centre
●	Ball carrier or receiver
◐	Player handling the ball for part of the play
▼	Defensive player
○——▼	Defensive player being blocked
→//	Fake possession of ball
→	Path of ball carrier or receiver
- - - →	Flight of tossed or passed ball
●——	Ball handed off

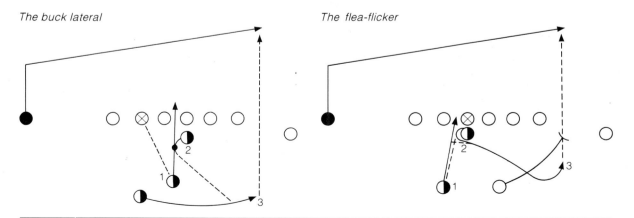

The buck lateral

The flea-flicker

the similarities between the two plays. Both involve feints into the line, and ball handling by several players, and conclude with a forward pass thrown to an end. Yet the first play, the 'buck lateral', pre-dates the second, the 'flea-flicker', by at least forty years!

Although some of the offensive systems which follow are now outmoded, they are included to demonstrate methods that offensive thinkers have devised over the years to outmanoeuvre, deceive, or overpower the defense. Today's theorists, having the advantage of hindsight, have produced far more sophisticated and precise offenses. But the objective remains the same – advance the ball and score points.

The single wing formation

The single wing formation derives its name from the position of the halfback or wingback outside the end. Most histories of the game credit Glenn 'Pop' Warner with the invention of this formation. He is best remembered for the teams he produced at Carlisle Indian School and Stanford University. The 'single wing' enjoyed tremendous popularity from the 1920s up until World War II, but was practically extinct by the mid-1950s.

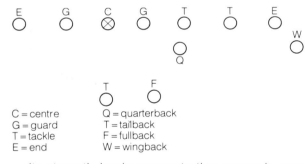

C = centre   Q = quarterback
G = guard   T = tailback
T = tackle   F = fullback
E = end   W = wingback

Its strength lay in concentrating power in one area by unbalancing the line and backfield. If the defensive men failed to compensate for the imbalance, they would be outnumbered and overpowered. On wide plays, guards and tackles pulled out of the line and led interference, clearing the way for the ball carrier.

Deception was added to power through the spinner play. In this play the ball was centred (tossed backward between the legs by the centre) to the fullback who would spin and hand-off to the tailback or fake the hand-off, continue the spin and carry the ball up the middle. The spin created a

delay which allowed a lineman to move laterally and trap a defensive man at the point of attack.

Single wing trap

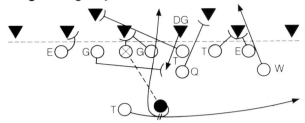

The ball is centred to the fullback who spins, pretending to give it to the tailback.

The defensive guard (DG) is lured into the trap by the offense allowing him unhindered passage across the line of scrimmage. Just as he is closing in on the apparently helpless ball carrier and contemplating a 'man of the match' award, the offensive left guard shatters his illusions with a bone crushing block from the side. Since the guard did not see the blocker, this is called a blind-side block and its victim is said to have been 'blind-sided'.

The would-be hero is now the goat. The fullback completes his spin, cuts off the left guard's block, and makes a nice gain.

Single wing buck lateral

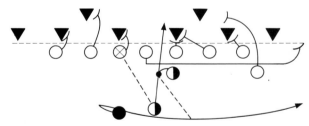

The ball is centred to the fullback. The fullback takes the ball straight ahead, giving it to the quarterback. The quarterback has turned to receive the ball and from that position he pitches to the tailback. The tailback has delayed his start by taking a short step to the left. This delay provides the time for the fullback-quarterback exchange.

The double wing formation

This was a contemporary of the single wing, also introduced by 'Pop' Warner. It was more deceptive

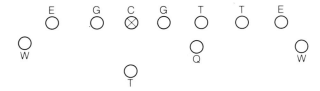

T = tailback
Q = quarterback
W = wing or halfback

Line positions identical
to the single wing

than the single wing because there was now a half- or wingback positioned outside of each end, so 'reverses' could be run in either direction. A reverse is a play starting toward one side of the field, which, through a ball exchange between backfield men, goes in exactly the opposite direction.

The double wing could also deploy four pass receivers in the least possible time.

Double wing reverse

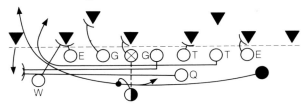

The ball is centred to the tailback, who spins and hands off to the right halfback. The tailback drives into the line, faking possession of the ball.

Note the number of blockers leading the play.

The spread or shotgun formation

Texas Christian and Southern Methodist Universities made the spread popular as a potent passing offense in the 1930s.

In the modern version, called the 'Shotgun', the quarterback lines up in his usual T formation position (see page 60), then shifts back to the tailback spot. The ball is centred to him with the old-fashioned between-the-legs toss. Since he is already in position to throw a pass, he has a better view of potential receivers and more time to select them.

Placing five eligible receivers where they can be found very quickly puts a great burden on the defense, but this offense lacks the speed and power often needed for an effective running game.

The spread is a good formation to employ when the offense has to pass and the defense knows it. Danny White, quarterback of the Dallas Cowboys, makes very effective use of this play, as did his predecessor, Roger Staubach.

Although not often done, it is possible to quick kick from this alignment and catch the defense napping.

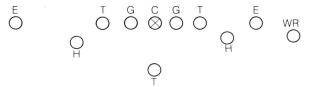

H = halfbacks
T = tailback or quarterback
WR = wide receiver or flanker

Offensive developments had an impact upon defensive thinking. The countermeasures which evolved in an attempt to neutralize offensive advantage are discussed in the section on defensive football.

Spread or shotgun (*pass or run*)

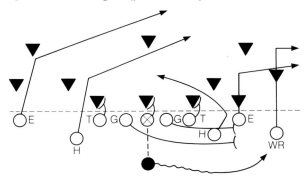

The quarterback is positioned about seven yards behind the centre. He takes a direct snap from the centre. The guards drop back to provide him with protection. This could be a run or a pass. Should the quarterback decide to run, the guards will lead the way.

The right halfback protects momentarily, then slides about three yards across the line. He provides a short outlet if a heavy rush is put on the passer by the defense.

This play, with five potential receivers and the run/pass option, places great pressure on the defensive safeties and cornerbacks.

The 'T' formation

This formation was first used prior to World War I. It was resurrected by the Chicago Bears in the late 1930s. Clark Shaughnessy of Stanford University introduced it into big-time college football in 1940.

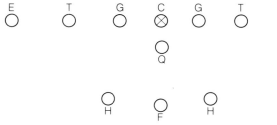

Q = quarterback
F = fullback/running back
H = halfback/running back

Super Bowl XX

The Bears scored twice in the 1986 Super Bowl on the basic T. Early in the game when close to the goal, they moved 'Refrigerator' Perry, their huge defensive lineman, to halfback.

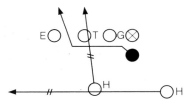

The odds were that Perry would carry on a dive, but McMahon, the quarterback, faked to him on the option, kept the ball, and cut off the tackle for a touchdown.

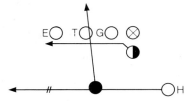

Later in a similar situation, the Refrigerator came in again. This time he was given the ball on the dive and went in for six points.

These plays were just as effective as when they were introduced in the 1940s.

Originally the back lined up in a formation resembling the letter 'T' with the quarterback set behind the centre. The centre handed the ball to the quarterback rather than tossing it as in the single wing. The term 'tight' T is used to describe this version because the players lined up in a close formation. Guards were one foot from the centre, tackles two feet from the guards and ends three feet from the tackles. The three backs were spaced at arm's length from each other.

Over the years, however, there have been many modifications, and now one seldom sees the four backs in the T position.

Along with the original version of the T formation (left), three of the most popular modifications are diagrammed. They are:

(1) The wing T, where one of the backs is placed outside the offensive end as in the single wing formation.

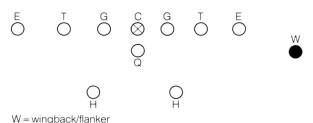

W = wingback/flanker

(2) The slot T in which an end is moved out two or three yards from his tackle and a back is placed in the slot or gap between end and tackle.

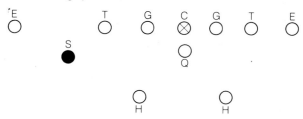

S = slotback

> 'Football authorities agree that of all the factors that produce success in a game, the proper selection of plays is by far the most important. A poor choice of plays will nullify the finest teamwork and will eventually break down the highest morale.'
>
> BOBBY DODD,
> GEORGIA TECH

(3) The pro set in which an end is spread to split at least ten yards outside his tackle and a back called a flanker or wide receiver is split about the same distance from the 'tight' end on the other side of the formation. The pro set is so-called because the professionals or 'pros' were the first to place or 'set' their players in this formation.

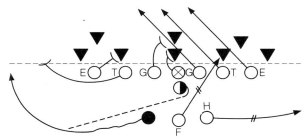

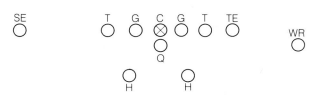

SE = split end
TE = tight end
WR = wide receiver/flanker

Regular T quick pitch or flip

The quarterback takes the snap from the centre, spins and pitches the ball to the left halfback who is breaking fast to the outside. The defensive end is not blocked, as the action is too quick for him to react in time to stop the play. The defensive men on the side away from the flow of the play are in the same situation and cannot pose a threat to the ball carrier; therefore, the linemen on that side release diagonally and block the first defensive back they encounter. (See first colour picture.)

The fullback and right halfback fake to hold the attention of the defense for a split second. A fake is as good as a block and infinitely more pleasant for the player executing it.

Should the defensive end drift to the outside, the pulling tackle will block him out, and the running back will cut inside. If not, the tackle turns the corner and heads upfield, blocking the first wrong colour jersey beyond the line of scrimmage.

An extra yard for Redskin Keith Griffin

The split T formation

The split T was developed during and immediately after World War II. Three of its leading exponents were the University of Missouri's Don Farout, Maryland's Jim Tatum, and Bud Wilkinson of Oklahoma University.

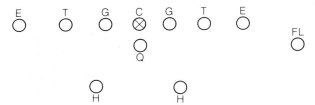

The linemen split much wider than in the normal T, encouraging the defense to split with them. Should the defense fail to split, the offense runs wide. As the defense moves out, large holes are left for inside plays. This concept can be likened to stretching a rubber band: the further the band is stretched, the thinner and weaker it becomes. The same principle applies to the defensive line.

The main feature of backfield play in the split T is called the 'option'. Here the quarterback moves along the line, either keeping the ball or pitching to a halfback swinging wide. Should the defensive end rush in, the quarterback pitches. If the end moves to the outside anticipating the pitch to the halfback, the quarterback fakes the pitch and cuts inside him, thus exercising his 'option'.

Split T option play

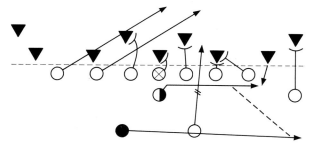

The quarterback takes the snap from centre and starts down the line. He puts a quick fake to the diving halfback. The defensive end is not blocked. The option for the quarterback depends upon the end's reactions. If he crashes at the quarterback, the pitch goes to the halfback swinging to the right. If the end tries to cover the halfback, the quarterback turns up inside of the end, keeping the ball.

The pitch on this option is very similar to the equivalent move in Rugby. American coaches who have the opportunity to play and observe Rugby anticipate that the British teams will employ more option plays than the average American team. This will take advantage of a skill that already exists in most British teams.

It puts tremendous one-on-one pressure on defensive men. In the Super Bowl XIX, the options run by quarterback Joe Montana made the difference in the game.

> 'When you're playing for the national championship, it's not a matter of life or death. It's more important than that.'
>
> DUFFY DAUGHERTY,
> MICHIGAN STATE

> 'When it comes to the football field, mind will always win over muscle and brute force.'
>
> WALTER CAMP,
> YALE UNIVERSITY

The 'I' formation

This formation originally placed the three backs in a straight line behind the quarterback, resembling an I, rather than a T.

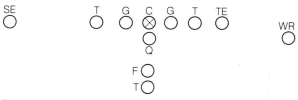

F = fullback
T = tailback

In the modern version, one of the backs and an end are split just as in the pro set. This alignment provides a blocking back in front of the tailback, who is the carrier on most running plays.

The professional tailback is allowed to choose his own route rather than running through a designated opening in the defensive line. This is called 'running to daylight'.

Bear Dennis Gentry breaking loose

'I' formation off-tackle power play

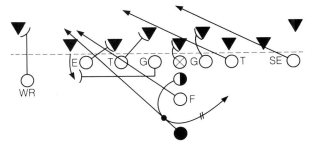

As the snap is taken by the quarterback, the left guard and fullback lead the play. The quarterback meets the tailback as he starts moving toward the hole. The left end and left tackle have good blocking angles which will make their assignments easier.

After the hand-off, the quarterback fakes as though he still has the ball and swings around to the right. This fake sets the stage for a subsequent play in which the quarterback actually keeps or 'bootlegs' the ball and throws a play action pass. In other words, the play is a pass which at the outset looks exactly like a running play.

Wishbone

The wishbone offense is still popular at the university level and Oklahoma used it in 1986 to gain the National Championship.

The position of backs is akin to an inverted 'T'. The advantage gained is that the point of the 'wishbone', the fullback, is close to the quarterback and gives the opportunity for an initial fake or play.

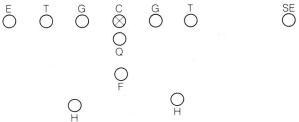

The offense requires a quarterback who is an expert at the option. Each and every play starts with the quarterback 'riding' the fullback at the off-tackle spot. He can give the ball to the fullback, follow it by giving to the second man, pitch to the third man going wide or go to a play action pass.

The disadvantage is that to be effective, it requires a full four-man backfield. This reduces the opportunity for fast release of receivers. Thus, the pros have used it only sparingly over the last few years.

Pro set pass play

On taking the ball from his centre, the quarterback drops straight back to elude the defensive charge. The interior linemen (centre, guards, and tackles) are assigned as his bodyguards. While the quarterback actually flees for his life, the bodyguards beat a strategic retreat, regrouping to form a protective zone around this VIP. The zone they form is known as the passing pocket or cup.

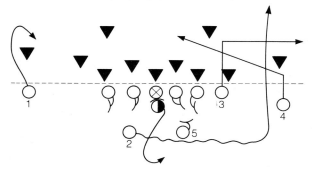

(1) The split end runs downfield twelve yards, stops, then turns sharply, coming back toward the quarterback. It is hoped his defender's backward momentum will prevent his reacting quickly enough to maintain coverage.

(2) The left halfback starts in motion before the ball is centred, then races (streaks) straight toward the goal posts (post pattern).

(3) The tight end runs downfield ten yards and cuts sharply toward the sidelines.

(4) The wide receiver proceeds five yards, then slants diagonally across the middle.

(5) The right halfback helps to protect the passer.

> 'The main thing is getting people to *play*. When you think it's your system that's winning, you're in for a damn big surprise. It's those players' efforts.'
>
> BUM PHILLIPS,
> COACH, HOUSTON OILERS

The quarterback looks for his primary or most logical receiver, the left halfback. Should this man be covered by the defense, the quarterback must choose a receiver from among the other three players running pass patterns.

Summary

The first question that the reader of this section should ask is: 'Why do teams keep changing these offensive formations; isn't there a finite number of plays the offense can call?' The reader may also wonder, 'What can the offense do to gain advantage of the defense?'

The following are some specific reasons for the different offenses. The reader should be able to go back and see how each offensive change was made for the purpose of trying to gain such advantages.

Power Certainly the offense, knowing where they are going, can concentrate power at one point. The single wing is the best example of this. Using the power 'I', an offense can still muster more muscle than a defense at a given point. Remember that the back is starting five to seven yards behind the line of scrimmage to gain speed. What is lost in distance is gained in speed!

Deception The quarterback can fake the ball to one back, then keep the ball and hand it to another back, or he may pass.

The option This is based on a Rugby manoeuvre and gives the quarterback the choice or option of doing two or more things depending upon the reaction of the defense. It generally involves a one-on-one situation between the quarterback and a defensive end.

Speed The invention of the T formation allowed the offense to take advantage of the defense with sheer speed. This was usually done with the halfback dive or a quick pitch around the end. Quick hitting was adequately demonstrated in the 1986 Super Bowl. Even though Refrigerator Perry was the halfback, he still hit the off-tackle spot with tremendous speed and went into the end zone standing up.

Reversing the flow When the offense starts in one direction, the defense must react. If it is a man in motion, the defense will usually cover with a single

Above: Rose Bowl tailgate party
Above right: The Rams marching band
Right: The Patriots cheerleaders

Previous page: Joe Theisman on the quick pitch
Below: Scoring the touchdown

Power overcoming a poor tackle

man adjustment. The defense will often anticipate the flow of the offense and overcompensate, throwing the ball carrier for a loss. The offensive team will then come back with a play which starts identically to the one thrown for a loss. This time the ball is given to a fast back who runs a reverse in exactly the opposite direction, catching the defense flatfooted. The same principle applies after an interior lineman has stopped a play by correct anticipation. In this case the play called is known as a counter or cross buck. The paths of the two backfield men involved, cross in a letter X.

Isolation and man-on-man This will be discussed in the section on passing. One example in the running game is with the deep tailback. A team with an exceptional running back will start him deeper so that he can evade the would-be tacklers one at a time. The runner has the advantage as he knows where he is going. The great runners like the Washington Redskins' John Riggins are spectacular in exploiting this advantage.

Red Grange

In 1926 Red Grange was voted on everybody's list as All-American while playing for the University of Illinois. That is, with the exception of the folks in Michigan. They had him on the second team. The University of Michigan Coach Yost remarked, 'Mr Grange will be carefully watched. Every time he gets the ball there will be eleven Michigan players facing him and stopping him.' Red's answer was on the field, as it should be for all great players.

Michigan kicked off, Red Grange took it in the air on his five yard line. He started to the left, got a block, reversed his field and went 95 yards for a touchdown.

The next time he got the ball on an end sweep. With a change of pace, he beat the cornerman and went 67 yards for the score.

After an exchange of punts, Red took the ball off-tackle. Following a block on the inside linebacker, he cut to the left and used his speed to go 56 yards for a touchdown.

On his next play, he went to the same 'hole' and through the secondary defense for a 46 yard touchdown. Red Grange had carried the ball four times in the first twelve minutes of play and he had scored four touchdowns. The coach pulled him out of the game at that point. The crowd gave him a standing ovation as he left the field.

In the fourth quarter the coach let him return to the field for one more play. He turned the corner and reached the end zone on a 19-yard carry. Five runs, five touchdowns and a total of 282 yards. The greatest individual performance in the history of the game.

'Football games aren't won … they're lost.'
FIELDING YOST
MICHIGAN COACH

Doug Flutie showing the perfect release

10 The passing game

The easiest way to gain yardage in football is with the pass. Yet, when you put the ball in the air, you gamble. You gamble with the elements, you gamble with your talent versus the opponents'. But you have the advantage of knowing what the play is to be and where it is going. The defense has the advantage of moving toward the action, against the pass.

As the quarterback drops back into the pocket, he will look in a neutral direction, but concentrate on his primary receiver. Three to five men will release to run what we call pass patterns. But the logistics of putting the ball in the air are fairly simple. There are usually under three seconds of protection available to the quarterback and one of those seconds is used in reaching the protective pocket.

If that primary receiver is covered, the quarterback 'pumps' a move in that direction (pretending to toss the ball) and then reverts to the secondary man. If that man is covered, you have a scrambling quarterback. The blockers cannot reasonably be expected to hold off the savage defense for more than three seconds. So if the

secondary receiver is not 'open', the quarterback will have to improvise by scrambling to avoid being tackled for a loss of yardage or, worse, bodily mutilation. Most quarterbacks find this situation disconcerting, but a few thrive on doubling as escape artists and pass with uncanny accuracy under these pressure conditions. Joe Montana, from San Francisco, is at his best under pressure. When all seems lost, he is the biggest threat to the defense. 'Scrambling' is a technique thought to have been invented by Minnesota Viking quarterback Fran Tarkenton, who gave his coach heart attacks and was nicknamed 'Fran the Scram'. He was extremely successful at it.

It must be appreciated, though, that the quarterback throws to a predetermined position most of the time. All of the short passes are position passes. The run, the cut and the pattern are measured in inches and micro-seconds.

The 'bomb', or long pass, is different. The ball is tossed with a 45 degree trajectory, nose up to float the ball, and the receiver runs *under* the ball. In observing the play, you will note that the receiver can usually beat the defense. It is reasonable to assume that the receiver can run faster forward than the defense can run backwards. But the measure of difference is usually less than a yard. Thus the receiver can't afford to telegraph the arrival of the ball. He must wait until the last minute to make his move.

Contact on the part of the defender is called 'pass interference', and has to be avoided. Once the ball makes contact, of course, all hell may break loose. The receiver is on the cross, and the defender is putting the nails in.

Bringing the ball in, stripping it away – that interchange is one of the most exciting moments in any game of Football.

Pass patterns

Following the snap of the ball, there are many possible routes or patterns that the receivers may take. Usually, the pattern is set by the quarterback. Sometimes the receiver is free to pick the best pattern. At other times the play will get 'busted' and the quarterback scrambles, looking for any open receiver.

Some very basic patterns are diagrammed. The names given are common but vary from team to team.

1. Delay
2. Slant-in
3. Hitch
4. Streak or Go
5. Post
6. Flag
7. Sideline
8. Break-in
9. Curl
10. Comeback

These patterns are diagrammed with the receiver on the left side of the ball. If the receiver were on the right side, the diagram would be mirrored.

The passing pocket

The quarterback, whether passing from the T or Shotgun formation, has two options. The first is to move with the backs and toss from a play action situation, meaning a pass that starts exactly like a running play. The second is the drop back pass in which he drops straight back into a protective zone or pocket.

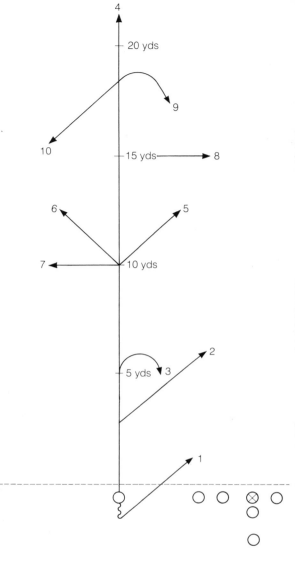

The professional quarterback represents a big financial investment, and it is hoped he will be able to run the team for many seasons. So he should not be exposed to unnecessary risks. Play action passes are dangerous because the quarterback is safe only as long as the defense thinks he does not have the ball. For this reason most professional teams employ the drop back. Even here the quarterback must get the pass away within three seconds.

Right: *Quarterback setting-up*

Although the concept of the passing pocket is simple, the techniques involved merit explanation. In creating the pocket, the guards and tackles have inside responsibility: they must not allow a defensive man through the gap to their inside (i.e. toward the middle of the line). If the halfbacks are not involved in the pass pattern, their assignment is to block rushers coming immediately outside the tackles. The object is not to lunge at the defenders but to hit, retreat, and regroup, continuing the process until the pass is thrown. The centre takes the man opposite and follows the same routine.

The quarterback drops back approximately seven yards, then steps forward into the safety of the pocket. By doing this he escapes from defenders zeroing in on him from the outside as their momentum prevents them from changing direction.

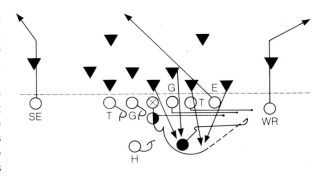

The quarterback now throws to the right half over the heads of the charging defenders. On catching the ball, the halfback shouts 'Go' and his three-man screen of blockers leads him downfield.

The two ends and the wide receiver run deep patterns to occupy the secondary defense.

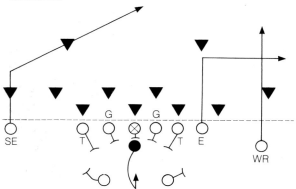

The defense, in an attempt to penetrate the pocket, will frequently run two men at one blocker. If he takes the man to the outside, the second man can slip into the pocket, spelling disaster for the quarterback.

The screen pass

The quarterback, fading to his right, drops back three steps. He fakes a throw and then turns and retreats to ensure that the defense, believing he is attempting to pass, will put on a hard rush.

The centre, right guard and right tackle block for two counts, release their men, and slide out five yards forming a screen. The right half blocks pass protection for two counts then moves up behind the screen. Meanwhile, the left side guard, tackle and halfback are actually protecting the passes.

The draw play

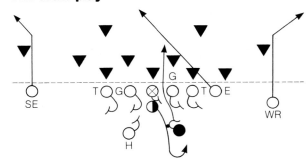

The quarterback drops back as if to pass, slipping the ball to the right half, who is in pass protection stance. The halfback maintains this stance until he sees an opening, then runs to daylight. The quarterback continues to drop back as if he still has the ball.

The line blocks as on a regular drop back pass. The receivers run deep patterns as they do in the screen pass.

STEVE FULLER,
Clemson quarterback, trying to decide on whether he should have a career in law or in football:

'You either have to finesse twelve people who weren't smart enough to get out of jury duty, or eleven who weren't smart enough to play offense.'

The play action pass

As it starts, this play appears to be the I formation power play off tackle. The quarterback fakes to the tailback who goes into the line as though he had the ball. Interior linemen cannot cross into the defensive secondary so they must block their men on the line of scrimmage.

The wide receiver runs across the field just behind the area formerly occupied by the linebackers, who should be moving toward the faking tailback. The tight end runs a post pattern while the split end 'streaks' (runs full speed straight toward the goal line). After completing the fake to the fullback, the quarterback keeps the ball hidden and swings around to his right. He then looks for an open receiver. (See photo below.)

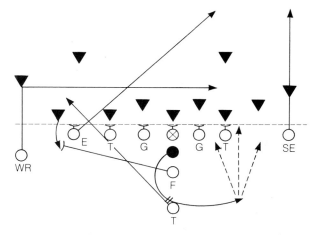

Inventor of the forward pass

John William Heisman coached from 1892 until 1927 at a number of different schools. As both player and coach he was a perfectionist. John was a short, stocky man with a handsome face ruined by a football-flattened nose. He ranks with Camp as an innovator and contributor to the game. Most outstanding of his contributions was the forward pass.

Heisman got the idea watching a game coached by 'Pop' Warner in 1895. Late in the game the fullback was running behind his scrimmage line looking for room to punt the ball. In desperation he just threw the ball downfield. A surprised teammate caught it and ran some seventy yards across the goal line. The officials allowed the play to stand. The touchdown counted, and the forward pass was now part of history.

Heisman saw immediately that the forward pass would open up the game and move it away from brute strength toward finesse and strategy. Little did he know that the ball would be reshaped for the passing hand, or what the professionals of today would do with this new weapon.

From 1927 until his death in 1936 he held the position of Athletic Director at the prestigious Downtown Athletic Club in New York City. In his memory, the club renamed their award the Heisman Trophy. It is given each year to the nation's outstanding college football player.

Left: *The cut – wrong-footing the defender*

The cut

In offensive football going for the ball on a pass is usually a matter of gaining a step on the defensive back. It requires that the receiving back or end makes a move or moves that separates him from the defense by that step or two. In the picture opposite, you will see a perfect example.

Note that the receiver in white has cut to his left while the defensive back is left in a position with his weight on his right foot. He obviously can't turn to stay with the receiver from that position.

The defensive man must make a full step so he can turn off his left foot to allow himself the opportunity to go to the right. Clearly the offensive receiver has the 'step advantage'.

It is the exceptional receiver who can approach a defensive man and force the above move. It requires reading the movement in micro-seconds. Yet, all the great receivers do it play after play.

The 'cut', the movement associated with the offensive receiver, is one of finesse. Mark Duper of the Miami Dolphins is exceptionally good at it.

Because of this move, some of the great receivers in the history of the game were able to compensate for a lack of exceptional speed. They didn't run past the defender, they 'cut' by him.

HEISMAN TROPHY

In 1975 Archie Griffin, running back for Ohio State, became the only person to win the Heisman Trophy twice, the highest accolade in College football.

Yet his size and lack of breakaway speed prevented him from becoming a successful back in the NFL.

Intestinal fortitude

11 Defensive football

'You attack each play with the intestinal fortitude that precludes concern for your own physical well being.'

ADE OLSON, COACH,
UNIVERSITY OF WISCONSIN, EAU CLAIRE

Six- and seven-man lines were standard defenses during the single wing era, but the speed and deception of the T, together with its passing threat, forced a change in defensive theory. Since the T did not rely on power blocking, it was now possible to employ fewer linemen and more defensive backs to protect against forward passes and pitches or options outside the end. The havoc created by the spinning, faking quarterback even caused some coaches to experiment with defenses in which the linemen were positioned a yard off the line of scrimmage. Although conceding a yard, it was felt that the extra distance between the two teams gave the defense a bit more time in which to analyze the play before committing themselves.

The stage was now set for the five-man line. In its earliest version there were three linebackers, one in the middle and two just outside the defensive tackles. There were two defensive halfbacks and a safety playing deep.

The emergence of the Split T with its option play placed the defensive end in an untenable position, so the 5–4 came into being. This defense placed a linebacker outside each end, allowing the end to go for the quarterback without worrying about the pitch to the halfback, who now became the responsibility of the outside linebacker.

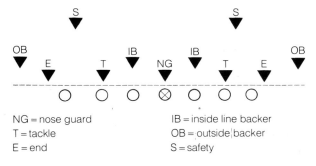

NG = nose guard
T = tackle
E = end

IB = inside line backer
OB = outside backer
S = safety

The advent of offenses with split ends and wide receivers posed such a passing threat that the two deep backs of the 5–4 could not cope. Therefore the outside backers were moved back several yards and renamed 'cornerbacks'. They were responsible for defending against passes and also for coming up to support the end on running plays.

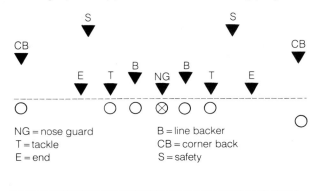

NG = nose guard
T = tackle
E = end

B = line backer
CB = corner back
S = safety

NG = nose guard
T = tackle
E = end

MB = middle backer
OB = outside backer
H = half back
S = safety

As professional teams continued to perfect the passing game, the defense was forced to make further adjustments which resulted in the three-man line so often seen on television. The players who were formerly at the end position are now dropped off as linebackers to defend against short passes, but at the same time they must be ready to move up to meet running plays.

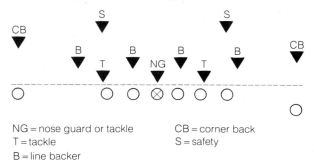

NG = nose guard or tackle
T = tackle
B = line backer
CB = corner back
S = safety

It is said that every action has a reaction. The truth of the saying is certainly illustrated in the evolution of defensive football. New offensive systems enjoy a spectacular but short-lived advantage because the defensive theorists soon develop ways of restoring the balance of power. When they succeed, the offensive thinkers go back to the drawing board and the cycle starts anew.

When watching the professionals play, one seldom sees a pure text book version of any defense because the professional offenses are so potent. Defenders at this level are faster and more versatile so defenses can be safely modified to cope with the particular strengths of the opponents' offense.

A quarterback may have a favourite receiver who merits extra coverage or there may be a particularly strong running back who must be contained. It is also possible that scouting reports indicate that a team consistently resorts to a certain play in a given situation. Modifications to cope with these cases are frequently accomplished by bringing safety men up to linebacker positions (the safety blitz), by dropping ends off the line to defend against short passes or by having linebackers retreat to cover passing zones or double up on receivers.

Most high school teams and their amateur equivalents would find it difficult to employ effectively the currently popular 3–4 defense as the two outside linebackers must be versatile enough to move up and play defensive end on running plays while being able to react quickly enough to cover receivers in the short passing zones.

Goal line defense

Any time the offensive team has the ball inside the ten yard line it is considered a goal line threat and most teams will modify or change their defense.

The 'gap-8', with a defensive lineman in each offensive gap, is a frequently-used defense in a goal-line situation. Since passes cannot be completed beyond the end zone there is less territory to cover. In theory it is expected that three men can cover the passing threat.

The eight-man front is difficult to penetrate as the defensive line now outnumbers the offensive line. The offense will generally attempt simple, fast developing plays as the blockers cannot keep a hole open very long against superior numbers.

Players in the diagrams are deliberately left unlabelled as the coach positions them according to where he feels they will perform best. Linebackers might be placed in the gaps on either side of the centre or they could be stationed in the positions normally occupied by the defensive ends. This would be sound stategy if the opponents often resorted to quick passes to the flat in short-yard-

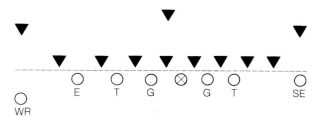

age situations, as linebackers can retreat and cover this area faster than the average defensive ends. The biggest, toughest defenders are usually placed in the gaps outside the offensive tackles where most power plays are directed.

The Bears 46 defense

This defense places ten men on or near the line of scrimmage. This puts tremendous pressure on the offense because as many as seven defenders may rush the quarterback. If the quarterback does not get rid of the ball quickly on passes, he will be swarmed under. On the other hand, if he can throw quickly, he has three receivers against only one defender, the safety.

The normal pass defense consists of four or five men rushing, with linebackers dropping off the line to cover the short pass zones.

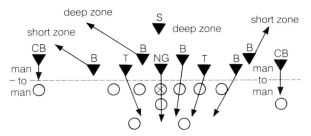

The ten-man front is in itself awe-inspiring, but the Bears made it even more effective by using stunts (unorthodox defensive movements) along with their regular rush. The example shown involved a linebacker who looped behind four charging defenders. They occupied the blockers while he slipped undetected into the pocket and tackled the passer for a big loss.

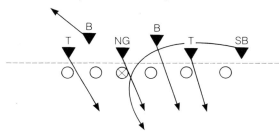

B = line backers
NG = nose guard
SB = stunting backer
T = tackle

This is a gambling defense which can backfire, but there are days when everything goes right. It was just such a day for the Bears in the 1986 Super Bowl.

Defensive stunt – the blitz

All teams employ stunts to confuse the blockers. They also 'overload' a point of the blocking screen. This stunt or overload is called a 'blitz'. The term is derived from the German *Blitzkrieg*, meaning lightning warfare. The main purpose of the blitz is to get to the quarterback for a 'sack' – dropping him for both a loss of yardage and loss of the down.

Danny White sacked!

Pass defense

The forward pass is such a potent offensive weapon that no discussion of defensive football would be complete without reference to defending against it.

On a passing play the defensive linemen pursue and harass the quarterback while the defensive secondary (linebackers, cornerbacks and safeties) must cover or mark the pass receivers – preventing them from catching the pass or tackling them immediately if they do. This section will deal with the activities of the latter group of defenders.

Man-to-man

The simplest method of defending against passes is 'man-to-man' coverage. This means that a defender is assigned to cover each eligible receiver, remaining with him regardless of route or pattern. It is easy to teach this method of coverage because it leaves no doubts about responsibility, but it breaks down when the receiver is too fast for the defender or outmanoeuvres him. There is no

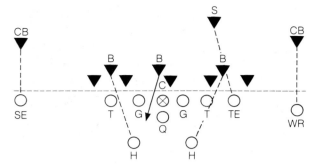

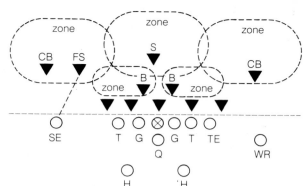

Left corner back – covers split end
Right corner back – covers wide reciever
Safety – covers tight end
Left backer – covers left half back
Right backer – covers right half back
Middle backer – blitzes

Safety = middle deep zone
Corner backs = outside deep zones
Line backers = short zones
Free safety – man-to-man on split end

one to assist the beaten defensive back when this happens.

Coverage is as follows: left cornerback covers the split end, right cornerback covers the wide receiver, safety covers the tight end, left backer covers the left halfback, right backer covers the right halfback, middle backer blitzes on the quarterback.

Zone defense

A second mode of coverage is the zone defense. Each defender is assigned a zone and required to cover any potential receiver who enters it. Zone boundaries cannot be marked on the field, so considerable drill is required before players are able to recognize their particular areas of responsibility. They must know precisely when a receiver enters a zone and when he leaves it to be covered by the man in the adjacent zone. This requires almost instantaneous judgment as well as oral communication between teammates while running full tilt.

By using four deep defenders and dividing the secondary into only three zones, it is possible to have one unassigned man called a 'free safety' who covers for mistakes made by the other three defensive men. Should the opponents have a particularly outstanding receiver, the free safety can follow him wherever he goes, thus achieving 'double coverage' (coverage of one man by the free safety in addition to the zone defender).

A favourite method of beating a zone defense is to overload one of the areas by sending two receivers into it. But if he is not involved in double coverage, an alert free safety will successfully counter this move.

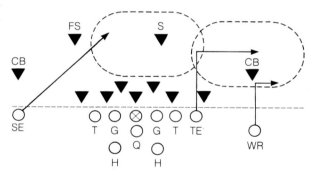

*Note that Safety cannot assist corner back in coping with two men as there is a man in his zone who must be covered

Another method is called 'splitting the seam', whereby receivers are sent into two adjacent zones, forcing the defenders to cover them. Meanwhile a receiver who has maintained a low profile by running half-speed or delaying his start, suddenly accelerates and slips into the seam or gap between the two defenders who are occupied elsewhere.

Considering the weaknesses of both systems, it would be impractical to rely exclusively on either man-to-man or zone defense. This is especially true in the professional game, where quarterbacks throw with pinpoint accuracy to glue-fingered

Double coverage

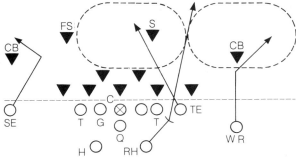

TIGHT END – runs through safety's zone drawing him to the left

WIDE RECEIVER – pulls corner back to the right with a sideline pattern

RIGHT HALFBACK – blocks end for two counts then slips into 'seam' between the zones being defended|by the safety and cornerback

SPLIT END – runs a pattern to occupy the free safety and corner back

receivers who were sprinters in their college days. One therefore finds various combinations of the two systems are employed by all the professional teams and the majority of the universities.

Summary of defense

The reader might sense that the defensive men have more fun. Football is a game of violence and for those who love contact, nothing could be better than being a linebacker. The ball carrier has to come in his direction to make yardage. There cannot be a more satisfying feeling than watching the 'hole' open to reveal the back with the ball. With the exception of using the facemask, practically anything goes in putting the ball carrier onto, or into, the ground.

The punt by Jeff Hayes

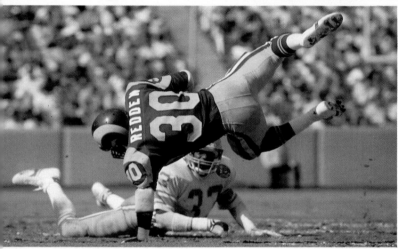

Above left: The proper way to carry the ball

Above: Quarterback ready from the top of the pocket

Left: Every which way but up!

Left: Marcus Allen fumbles

Overleaf: Gang-tackling Payton

12 The kicking game

'Football' is probably a misnomer when applied to the American version of the sport, but kicking is still an important part of the game, especially when one considers the number of games won or lost in the last seconds by a field goal, blocked punt or fumbled kick-off.

In the early years the punt was considered an important strategic weapon, used to keep the opponent deep in his own territory. By keeping the opposition near his goal, a fumble, pass interception or blocked punt could lead to an easy touchdown for the defensive team. As offensive techniques improved and the forward pass was more widely used, it became easier to score from any position on the field. Thus, the punting game declined.

It has been noted already that the evolution of the shape of the ball made it easier to handle and to pass, yet harder to kick. Many of the longest field goals were kicked with the older and rounder ball. The total volume of the ball decreased, with the weight remaining about the same. Things like density and specific gravity are not normally discussed in football circles, but in basic terms, the bigger ball 'floated' more and thus could be kicked a greater distance. The more compact ball could be passed with greater accuracy.

The kick-off

The kick-off, as we have seen, starts every game. The officials flip a coin and the winner of that flip has the choice of kicking or receiving the ball. The team winning the toss will generally choose to receive, but exceptions may occur. If a team feels it is capable of stopping the opponents and forcing them into surrendering the ball, it might choose to kick. Wind, rain, or slippery turf should also be considered when choosing whether to kick or receive.

The kicking team's objective, with one exception, is to kick the ball high and deep, enabling their men to get down under it and tackle the receiver close to his own goal line. The exception occurs when the kicking team's side is behind late in the game. They must maintain their squad's possession of the ball, and this can be accomplished by a crafty short kick. The difficult-to-handle ball, after travelling ten yards, may legally be recovered by the kicking team themselves, instead of the 'enemy' receiver. This is called the 'onside kick' rule.

The two illustrations following are examples of a kick-off. The first is the American style, where the toe is kicked straight into the ball. The second is called a 'soccer' or 'European' style kick, where the foot comes across the ball. Because so much more power can be generated by the soccer kick, it is now used by most kickers.

American-style

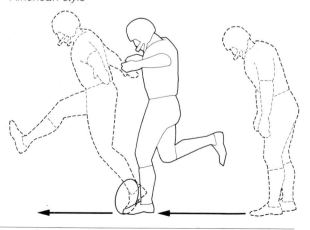

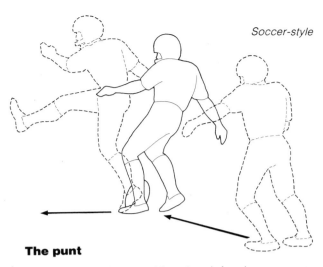

Soccer-style

The punt

The punt can be considered a defensive weapon; it is generally kicked high and deep. This enables the kicking team to get downfield and make the tackle close to the opponents' goal.

There are times, however, when to avoid kicking into the end zone the punter will angle the ball out of bounds as close as possible to the goal line. This 'coffin corner' kick is used to avoid giving the ball to the opponents on their own twenty yard line. (See touchback in glossary.) Another reason for the out-of-bounds kick is to keep the ball away from a dangerous runner. (Kicking to the weakest receiver is a wise practice, but it should be remembered that if the opponents run a reverse, whereby the ball carrier gives the ball to a teammate going in the opposite direction, the stronger receiver may end up returning the kick.) The ends release quickly and are responsible for preventing a return up the sidelines which offer an easy route for a touchdown.

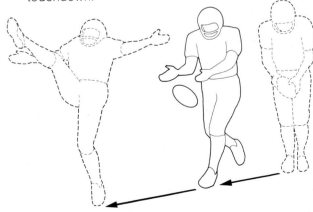

Punt formation

The tight and loose formations are those commonly used. The kicker in the tight punt is placed ten yards deep, and the linemen take normal splits. (This, as already explained, means that the feet of the guard are about one foot from the centre, the tackles about two feet from the guards and the ends about three feet from the tackles.) Each is responsible for preventing anyone getting through the gap to his inside, and a defender going around this wall will be too slow to bother the kicker. The ends bump the man to their inside, then proceed downfield to cover the return. Interior linemen and backs continue to protect the kicker until they hear the thump of the ball before proceeding downfield. The kicker holds back and acts as a safety.

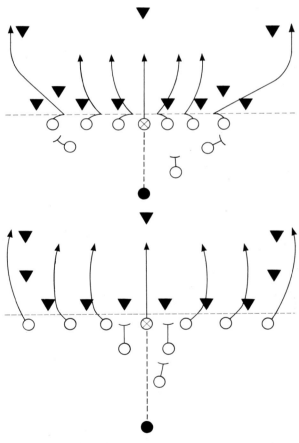

The kicker in the loose formation lines up so deep (approximately fifteen yards) that it is practically impossible for a defensive player to reach him in time to prevent the kick. Since less protection is needed, the linemen are able to spread out and obtain better coverage of the return. Each interior lineman is responsible for the gap to his outside and only bumps his opponent before taking off. The ends release immediately on the snap.

The punt return

The return of the punt can provide the opportunity to score an easy touchdown. The key to making it the big play is getting more blockers than defensive men into one area. Opposite is an example of overloading the left sideline with a wall of blockers. If the receivers can lure the tacklers from the kicking team toward the centre of the field, the chances for a touchdown are excellent.

Notice that both of the deep return men move to the centre of the field after the catch. The man with the ball will be giving ground while going for the outside lane. If the kick went to the receiver on the right, they could converge in the middle, pass the ball, and run a reverse off the punt. In the diagram the actual receiver merely fakes giving the ball to his teammate.

Note in the photo that the blockers in the dark shirts, numbers 72, 78, 66, and 80 have set up

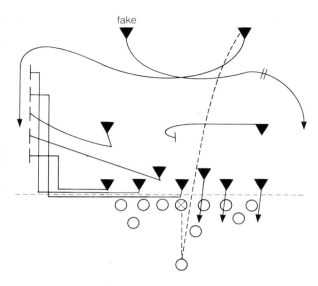

the 'wall'. But the receiver did not get to the other side, near the sideline. Thus, the picture gives a perfect example of a play gone 'bust'. That wall of blockers really can't do a thing for the ball carrier in that position. Had he managed to get to the other side of the 'wall', those men would have been in a perfect position to execute blocks and he might have gone the distance for a touchdown.

The field goal

This part of the kicking game is becoming even more important due to improving defenses which keep the offense away from the goal line. Attempts are made from a greater distance and more often than before. Scoring from field goals and point-after-touchdowns accounts for more than fifteen per cent of all points scored.

The important elements in field goal kicking are centring of the ball, the holder, the blocking and, of course, the kicker. The centre must look between his legs to spot the holder. This places him at a big disadvantage in trying to block the defensive nose guard in front of him. On the snap of the ball the other offensive linemen move toward the centre, forming a wall to prevent a defensive breakthrough which could result in a blocked kick.

The holder plays a most important role, as there

A punt from the loose formation

are less than two seconds between the snap from centre and placement of the ball.

All blocking is with inside responsibility to form a 'cup' similar to that used in pass or punt protection.

Most kickers now use the soccer style kick. The reader should refer back to the two illustrations for the kick-off (pages 81 and 82). The style of kick can be the same for both the field goal and the kick-off, the difference being that on the kick-off the ball is set on a 'tee'. With the field goal the ball

Field goal attempt

is spotted about twelve yards behind the centre and put into position by the holder. That holder is usually the quarterback. He is normally the best ball-handler and passer on the team.

It is easy to see how this keeps the defense 'honest' (i.e. unable to make any sly advance plans). They cannot all rush the kicker, because of the potential threat of a pass or other play.

Quarterback rolling out

13 Anatomy of a play

Unlike soccer and Rugby manoeuvres, the plays, as they are known in American Football, are pre-arranged and rehearsed. There is relatively little 'freelancing' once the centre delivers the ball to the quarterback.

On each play, every member of the offensive team has a definite assignment in which he either handles the ball, carries the ball, fakes as if he is getting the ball, blocks a defensive man, or runs a pass pattern.

The plays are named and numbered so that the quarterback going into the huddle need only give some very basic information for the team members to identify their individual assignments. Those individual assignments constitute a committed assault at a predetermined point of the defense.

The offense never tries to beat the total defense. They try to isolate a point of attack. Coaching comes into play then. The defense will make an adjustment, and the offense will try to adjust to that adjustment. It is really a game of chess, with eighteen-stone men making the moves.

The quarterback will first give some unique assignments, such as telling an end to 'split' and a back to move into a flanker position. He will follow that direction with an indication of the flow or backfield movement. Then he will give some key numbers that will tell everybody who will carry the ball and where.

The following is a typical numbering system used to design the pattern of plays. The slots between the linemen are numbered and the backs are numbered.

The coach can also assign the number to the linemen rather than to the slot between the men.

Coaches have invested hours, seasons and careers arguing about the best way to number the offense. Either way is acceptable. The first is better for power plays and the second is better for quick hitting plays. The two-digit number assigns the back to a hole in the line. Number 24 means the number 2 back is carrying the ball at the number 4 hole. The term 'hole' is used because it is presumed that the offensive men will block the defense and create a 'hole' for the ball carrier to run through.

So the viewer now starts with a balanced T-formation. The quarterback steps into the huddle and says, 'Split right, flanker left.' This sets the formation.

The number 3 back is flankered to the left; he is now in the position of a wide receiver. The right end moves out; he is now called either a split end or wide receiver.

He then says, 'Dive right.' This determines the flow of the backfield.

Then he says, '24 on 2.'

That means the number 2 back at the number 4 hole and the play will start on the count of two. When the quarterback takes his position behind the centre he calls out signals to indicate the time to centre the ball. Most teams go with the preliminary sound 'Hut!' So the quarterback will say, 'Hut-one, Hut-two, Hut-three,' etc. On the 'Hut-two' the ball is handed to the quarterback and the action starts.

The quarterback has his hand on the centre's bottom, pushing forward to maintain contact. His other hand is below the first and the centre places the ball firmly into the two hands. When the quarterback gets the ball, he steps forward at a diagonal and starts down the 'line'. The right halfback (running back on the right) dives straight ahead and takes the ball from the quarterback.

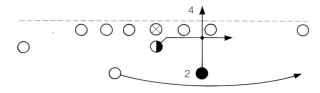

The left half runs a sweep pattern to his right and fakes as if he is getting the ball from the quarterback. Assuming that the defense is a 3–4, the blocking assignments would be as indicated in the diagram.

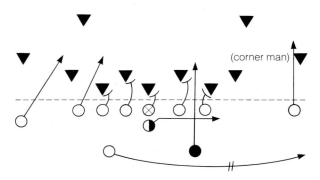

If the play is successful, they might run it again. However, all teams have look-alikes or 'patterns' to keep the defense confused. An example would be for the quarterback to call a 'split right, flanker left, dive right, 18.'

Everybody does the same thing as on the 24, but the ball is faked to the number 2 back and pitched to the number 1 back going round the end.

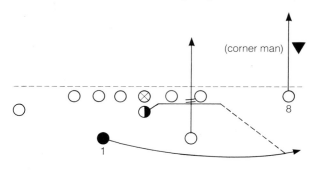

On the next play the quarterback might call a 'split right, flanker left, dive right, hook pass.' He would fake the hand-off to the number 2 back, fake a pitch to the number 1 back and toss a pass to his split right end.

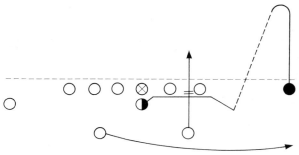

All three of these plays would start out looking the same. If you were the corner man on that 3–4 defense, you could get totally frustrated. As Bart Starr said about his coach, Vince Lombardi, 'He's the only man I know that can swear using words like "golly, gosh and darn"!' The cornerman says 'golly' when the 24 is inside him, 'gosh' when the 18 sweeps outside him and 'darn' when the hook is caught in front of him.

For the novice, this might sound very complicated. It is simpler if one knows that 'split right' only affects the right end. 'Flanker left' only affects the number 3 back. The 'dive right' is for the two backs. The '4' in '24' tells the linemen where to block, and the '2' in '24' tells the number 2 back he is getting the ball. With the same formation, this series of plays could be run to the left by simply mirroring all assignments.

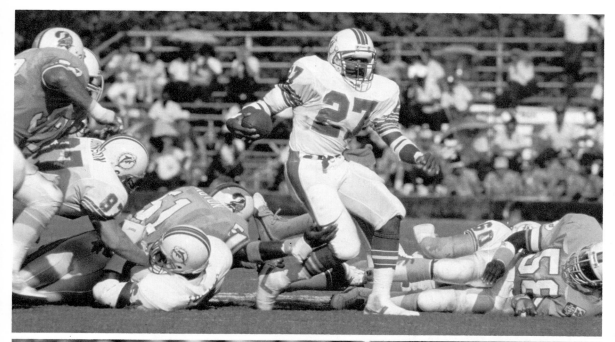

Clearing the line of scrimmage (top) *and getting nailed* (below)

The Raiders cheerleaders take over the Olympic Stadium

14 Behind the scenes

The reader now has an understanding (we hope!) of the terms, formations, penalties and procedures. This chapter deals with what goes on behind the scenes. This will enable the reader normally cast in the role of spectator to see the game from different points of view.

As can well be imagined, spectators are a mixed bunch. Some are there to see their first game, others have played and coached and for sure some of the 'old pros' are still there, too, enjoying the combat of mind, muscle and speed.

The spectators in the States arrive for the game at a variety of times, some just making it in time for the kick-off and others camped out in the parking lot the night before. The players usually try to avoid meeting with the fans and the press prior to the game, for two reasons. One, they don't want to be put off their game or lose concentration and two, they have other fish to fry, though of course the big names and coaches have to do their part in public relations and press conferences.

One of the first things the quarterbacks and coaches will do is to walk the field. Even in a dome where there is artificial turf, the surface and light can vary at different places on the field. When the turf is natural - and more so when the field is used for other sports such as baseball – an understanding of the varying conditions is most important.

In the locker room each and every player develops his own ritual of getting ready. First there is a check of the equipment: no player wants a broken lace to ruin his chances. The surface of the field and the weather will determine what type of shoe to wear. Some players will go out and test the field surface. The assistant coaches will check the telephone and 'spotting' communications. In every game, some of the coaching staff are located high in the stadium for an unobstructed view. They are tied into the defensive co-ordinator, the offensive co-ordinator and the head coach by telephone. When you see the coach with headphones on, he isn't listening to his stereo.

'Be more concerned with your character than with your reputation, because your character is what you really are, while your reputation is merely what others think you are.'

TOM LANDRY,
COACH, DALLAS COWBOYS

Players with injuries, and this is almost everyone by the mid-season, will have a trainer or doctor patch them up. Routinely, every player has his ankles taped. This gives support that the shoes don't provide, and without much additional weight. Jammed and injured fingers get taped together, usually the wrists get taped and yes, some tape is applied for psychological reasons.

The coaches move about the locker room talking with each individual player. They review special assignments. They discuss replacements and substitutes in the event of an injury. Special teams (those little groups you see running on the field for particular play situations) are reidentified. Some of those teams are used for kick-offs, punting, field goals, and goal line defenses. There are also 're-finement' special teams. These involve changing only two or three players. For example, if it is clearly a long pass situation, the offense might pull a tight end and a running back out of the game and replace them with two good wide receivers. At the same time the defense will pull big linemen and replace them with faster linebackers, cornermen or safeties to give them more strength against the pass. Remember, in the game there are only thirty seconds between plays, so very little time for discussion. Those reviews in the locker room are necessary before each game.

The quarterback and the head coach will then review the 'game plan'. This plan is a result of untold hours of watching films of the opposing team, reviewing statistics, updating their knowledge of the opposing teams' injuries and any other information that could play a part. They approach the game with specific ideas of how the opposition will act and react. One team might be going for the fast and easy touchdown, the other might be playing a ball control offense. Teams usually stay with their game plan unless something drastic forces them to alter it.

Just prior to leaving the locker room, the captain and head coach will usually share a thought with the team. For the most part this is intended to be inspirational as the game is played on emotions as much as any set of muscles. There may be a team prayer.

When they take the field, usually twenty minutes before the kick-off, players in the pros tend to warm-up on their own. In the schools and colleges this warm-up is more formalized with everybody doing roughly the same thing. The captains are then called to the middle of the field for the flipping of the coin. (The winner will have the choice of kicking or receiving.) Then there is that moment of truth when the local band plays the National Anthem. We Americans, you may have noticed, are very patriotic! Within sixty seconds the ball is in the air, and the game is on.

To appreciate and understand the game, it is necessary to be aware of the tactical situation prior to each play. What is the down, yardage to go, time remaining, score, field position, etc.? One frequently hears comments regarding a team's ability to 'convert on third down', referring to whether or not they are capable of making the 'big play' and a first down. If they haven't got it in them, they must surrender the ball by punting on fourth down.

As an example, say the offensive team has the ball on their own forty-yard line with a third down and eight yards to go. They lead by five points, and there are seven minutes remaining in the game. It is essential that they retain possession of the ball. If the next play does not produce the required yardage, they will be forced to punt, thus giving their opponents the ball and another chance to score. The defensive team will therefore be anticipating a play designed for a considerable gain. A dive or power play off tackle would not be a good choice, but completion of a medium-range pass would gain the necessary yardage.

Knowing that the defense is aware of the passing threat, the quarterback may elect to run a draw play up the middle or a screen pass over the heads of the hard-charging defenders who have predicted their defense on the probability of a regular drop-back pass.

In a 'third down and two' situation, the dive or power play is a logical choice. However, a shrewd quarterback, realizing that the defense is anticipating just such a call, may select something completely different. He must weigh the odds. Are the chances of making the required yardage in the obvious way better than if he resorts to the unexpected? If so, he goes with the obvious. There is no such thing as a right call. Truth in football, as in pragmatic philosophy, is relative. So much depends on time and place. If a thing works, use it.

Field position is another consideration. If the

Attempting to reach the sidelines to stop the clock

offensive team has the ball deep in its own territory, it needs to move upfield pretty carefully to avoid the possibility of a safety or a blocked punt. This is no place for slow-developing trick plays, requiring lots of ball handling and the chance for a fumble. Simple, quick-hitting plays are in order. A deep drop-back pass is permissible, as the quarterback can always throw the ball away if his protection breaks down.

Between the thirty-yard lines anything can be expected. Here the quarterback feels free to display his wares. Proximity to the enemy goal, however, once again limits the choice of plays. This is simply because the defensive team, having a smaller area to defend, is able to consolidate its forces and use more men in the line of scrimmage. (Refer to the item on goal line defense.) Quick-hitters are wise choices, especially flips to the outside. Play action passes are also effective.

The time factor is also crucial. A team leading in the last quarter will try to keep the clock running and stay away from the sidelines. If the ball carrier is forced out of bounds, the clock is stopped and the defense gets a new lease on life. Conversely, if the offensive team is behind, they will do everything possible to stay near the sidelines and stop the clock at every opportunity.

Knowing the coach's approach to football adds to the viewer's enjoyment by enabling him or her to anticipate strategy as the game progresses. Some

> 'It's a game in which you can feel a clean hatred for your opponent.'
>
> RONALD REAGAN,
> FORMER SMALL COLLEGE FOOTBALL PLAYER

coaches feel that the best defense is a good offense, while others, such as the Chicago Bears' coach, place great emphasis on creating a defensive unit which intimidates the offense, thus forcing mistakes and turnovers. There are winning coaches who use a wide open, gambling offense, and there are others with equally good records whose systems are based upon ball control and playing the percentages.

The best coaches are no doubt those who fit their system to their material. This practice is in keeping with the advice of President Theodore Roosevelt, a great advocate of the rugged life. 'Do what you can, where you are, with what you have,' was his motto.

The role of the coach

In general the American Football coach, especially the head coach, is a more authoritarian figure than his British counterpart. Perhaps his proximity to the players during the game is a factor. He sends in substitutes with messages, talks to players on the bench, and can even bring his entire team to the sidelines during time-outs. The instinct of self-preservation might also foster the authoritative attitude. Since the tenure of coaches at all levels depends greatly upon won-lost records, it follows that the coach will demand authority commensurate with his responsibility.

Tradition casts the coach in the role of teacher, father-figure, public relations man, and master strategist. As a teacher, he must ensure that his team is fundamentally sound and reinforce this with constant drill so that the players can react automatically in the emotionally charged atmosphere of the game. If the team does not understand and execute fundamentals instantly, all the coach's rhetoric, strategy and deceptive plays are to no avail.

There are many tales about the great coach, Vince Lombardi, treating veteran Green Bay players as wayward children. George Halas, founder and long-time coach of the Chicago Bears, earned the nickname 'Papa Bear' by establishing much the same relationship with his players. At the high school and college levels the coach assumes the surrogate father role to an even greater degree.

The public and the players expect the coach to conduct himself with dignity and to control his emotions in situations where the entire stadium is in a state of bedlam. In occupying such a visible position his actions are easily observed and often televised. The coach is held responsible for his team's behaviour on and off the field, as well as for strategic and tactical errors during the game. More often than not he is expected to transform mediocre talent into a winning team ... and is sacked for not so doing.

He operates as supreme commander from the sidelines but has an *alter ego* on the field of play in the person of the quarterback.

History records the famous quote attributed to the University of Notre Dame coach, Knute Rockne. When playing a weaker side, Michigan, his team was behind 14–0 at half-time. He had not said a word during the fifteen-minute break until it was time for them to return to the field, whereupon he gave vent to his feelings: 'All right girls, let's go!' Notre Dame beat Michigan 34–14.

The quarterback

It is generally accepted that the quarterback is the most important man on the field. Since one of your authors had the good fortune to play this position for eight years it is felt that an analysis of the mental and physical requirements would be of value to the reader.

Initially the quarterback must be a leader and have the confidence of his teammates. He in turn must have confidence in his coach. He must have a studious approach to the game, knowing not only his own responsibility on the play, but that of every other offensive player. This is true on each and every play. Should a play fail through a missed assignment, the quarterback must be able to identify and correct the error. Should it fail because

---

'There has never been a success story in football or any other endeavour without pride being the keynote. As complex as the subject is, the coach should constantly search for young men with built-in pride, and then strive to develop and sustain it.'

VINCE DOOLEY
UNIVERSITY OF GEORGIA

A strong arm and the ability to throw
an accurate forward pass

of a new defensive alignment or manoeuvre, he must recognize the threat and select plays to counter it.

Infectious confidence and enthusiasm are essential. When he calls a play the quarterback's teammates should feel that he has just revealed the greatest piece of strategy since Nelson's battle plan at Trafalgar – perhaps an overstatement, but one doubting teammate can mean a 'busted assignment'. He must thrive on competition and take defeat, while accepting it gracefully, as a personal insult. (Joe Thiesman of the Washington Redskins exemplifies this aspect of leadership.) Realizing that his glamour role has a price tag, he must be willing and able to accept criticism from the coach and fans. He will receive just as large a share of the blame for defeat as he will the glory of a victory.

Mental attributes take precedence but certain physical qualities are vital. Probably the most important is a strong arm and the ability to throw an accurate forward pass. Accuracy is more significant than distance. A clear, calm communicating voice is a requisite. The quarterback must be heard above the noise of the crowd, while instilling confidence in nervous teammates. Great speed is not required but co-ordination and 'good hands' are. The quarterback handles the ball on every play, spinning, faking, handing off or passing while executing footwork as intricate as a dance routine.

The tailgate party

The term 'tailgate' refers to the fifth door on those large American station wagons popular in the Fifties and Sixties. Fans pull into the parking area next to the football stadium and from the tailgate they bring forth a picnic lunch before the game. In the finest American tradition, if a little lunch is good, a bigger one is better. Soon the lunch of yesteryear became brunch and now, as you may gather, some recreational vehicles arrive the night before the game. At the universities even more than at the pro games, the fans make the football a full-day event. The dress, the hats and the fanfare are reflective of the home team's uniform and colours. Barbecue grills are set up, kegs of beer tapped and that picnic lunch is now a full blown banquet. (See colour picture.)

Qu'est-que-ce?

Chefs and would-be chefs take tremendous pride in the meal they are able to produce in the parking lot (out of the tailgate). Microwave ovens are employed, along with other modern technology. The Americans, especially the Texans, think they have invented something new, though a visit to Henley-on-Thames during the regatta soon dispels this illusion. The tailgate party has been going on there for a hundred years, even if the meals served are smaller, with more crystal, more silver and yes, more class.

On a very positive note the American fan is there to cheer his team in victory and to find humour in defeat. American Football has really never known any hooliganism. The fans themselves are part of the game. On the rare occasion the cheerleaders will be passed hand over hand from the field up into the stands, around, and back down, but none the worse for wear. Some of the cheers and chants denote the humour of spectators doing their best to support a losing team.

More than fifty?

> *We're so neat*
>   *we're so nifty,*
> *We don't lose*
>   *by more than fifty*

is a favourite; or when the opposing team is on another touchdown march,

> *Retard them,*
>   *retard them,*
> *make them*
>   *relinquish the ball!*

is particularly popular. The spirited fan, boasting a smattering of French, might even hope for a turnover:

> *Qu'est-que-ce?*
>   *Qu'est-qu-ce?*
> *Take the ball the other way!*

The tailgate party and the cheers and chants have become a very important part of the American Football scene.

The day the band got on the field

In 1982, the big game between California and Stanford was almost over. With Stanford leading by two points, Cal had time for one more play.

The famous Stanford Marching Band was on the sidelines waiting to do their end-of-game performance. Just as California's offensive team started their last play (which was a play action pass), the Stanford band came marching on the field prematurely. With the play already in progress, the Cal backfield started to use the band members as screens for their offensive attack. Exchanging the ball on five different laterals, the California team went the length of the field and scored. Snatching victory from defeat, they won 25–20.

It is not known what happened to the band director.

Marcus Ailen hurdling

15 Glossary

AUDIBLE   A secret word and/or number used by the quarterback to change the play at the line of scrimmage to exploit a weakness in the defense.

BACK   A member of either the offense or the defensive team who is positioned off the line of scrimmage. On offense the back may carry the ball.

BALANCED ATTACK   Refers to a team using both its running game and its passing game to make effective yardage. This is important, because otherwise the defense can adjust its formations against the anticipated approach.

BALANCED LINE   This is when the centre is actually in the centre! He will have a guard, tackle and end on each side of him.

BALL CONTROL   The team that has the advantage of a lead or position will try to retain the ball for as long as possible. It will run more plays and pass less. This keeps the ball in possession, and can be a total game plan.

BLIND SIDE BLOCK   A block that is unexpected and unseen by the player being blocked.

BLITZ   A defensive manoeuvre in which one or more of the defense players change their responsibilities and rush the quarterback, hoping for a sack.

BLOCK   To retard the movement of a defensive player with legal body contact. A player must use the upper body, and if the arms are used, they must be close to the body. The move is designed to keep the tackler from the ball carrier.

BLOCKED KICK   A stopped or deflected try-for-point, punt, or field goal.

BOMB   The name given to the last-resort long pass. It usually results in nothing, but can produce the long touchdown.

BOOTLEG   This is a play where the quarterback fakes a hand-off, puts the ball on his hip and tries to go in the other direction, undetected.

BROKEN FIELD RUNNING   Refers to the position of the ball carrier on a punt return, kick-off return or on a long run. The ball carrier is footloose in open field and can therefore approach the oncoming defensive men one at a time.

BROKEN PATTERN   This is when the receiver realizes that the quarterback is in trouble. He breaks to any position on the field where he might be identified as open to get the pass from the quarterback.

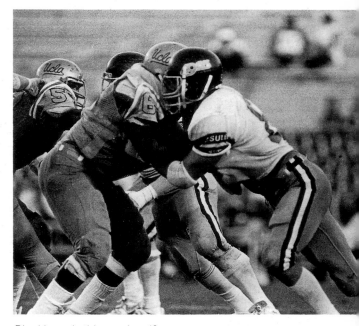

Blocking – is this one legal?

BRUSH BLOCK   This is a partial block to provide a short delay of a defensive player. Often used by receivers prior to releasing for a pass.

BUCK   A play going straight into the line.

BUTTON HOOK   (Curl Pass) The receiver starts straight downfield then turns 180 degrees to face the passer as the ball is thrown.

CENTRE   The person who snaps the ball. Also, the process of putting the ball in play.

CHAIN   This is a ten-yard chain between two poles used to measure the distance required by the offense.

CHAIN CREW   The three-man, sideline crew keeping the chain and down marker. They indicate the start of the first down, the end of ten yards and present location of the ball. The marker indicates the next down.

CHUCKING   A defensive move used to keep the blocker away from the body of the defender: a push with the hands, release, and another push. This leaves the defender free to pursue the ball carrier.

CLIPPING   To block or hit a player from behind. Illegal, unless it is the ball carrier or takes place close to the line of scrimmage.

CLOTHESLINING   This is where a defensive player will swing an arm in an arc to make contact with the face, head or neck of an offensive player. The result is the same as a person running full speed and catching his neck on a clothesline.

COLLEGE DRAFT   A system set up by the NFL to share the wealth of talent coming out of the universities each year. The teams have a rotating choice of the players. The team with the worst record gets the first choice, and so on. The first-year player is called a rookie. The rookie has no choice as to which team he will play for that first year.

COMPLETED PASS   A forward pass that is legally caught. If it is caught by the opposition, it is called an interception.

CONVERSION   This is the try-for-point after a touchdown. If the kick is good, it scores one point.

CORNERBACK   A defensive player who lines up outside the end and a couple of yards deep. He must cover both the run and the pass. Most coaches consider this the most difficult position on defense.

COUNT   The quarterback calls out signals to start a play, usually in a pattern like: 'Hut-1, hut-2, hut-3!'

COUNTER PLAY   A play where the flow of the backfield goes in one direction and the ball carrier goes in the 'counter' or opposite direction.

COVERAGE   This is a term given to the pass defense – how receivers are marked or covered. Basic styles are man-to-man and zone.

CRACKBACK BLOCK   Occurs when a receiver turns back against the defense and throws a downfield block. To be legal it must be above the waist.

CRAWLING   Attempting to advance the ball after being tackled and the play whistled dead.

CROSSBAR   The horizontal bar in the goal posts.

CUP   The offensive blocking pocket for passing, punting and field goals.

CUT   Any change in direction by a ball carrier or receiver.

CUT-OFF BLOCK   A block where an offensive player will get between the defensive man and the ball carrier. Often contact is not even made, but he cuts off the path to the ball carrier.

DEAD BALL   The ball that is no longer in play or 'live' after the whistle is blown.

DEEP MAN   The receiver who runs the longest or deepest pass pattern.

DEFENSE   The team that does not have the ball. They are defending their goal, trying to prevent the offense from reaching it.

DEFENSIVE BACKFIELD   A four-man unit consisting of two cornerbacks and two safeties.

DEFENSIVE HOLDING   Illegal use of the hands while blocking an offensive player.

DEFENSIVE LINE   The two tackles, two ends, and nose guard.

DELAY OF GAME   Any action – or inaction – by either team which prevents the ball from being put in play promptly.

DIRECT PASS   A pass from the centre to a backfield man or other player positioned several yards behind the line of scrimmage, as in the case of the centre's pass to the punter.

DISQUALIFIED PLAYER   A player who is banished from the game for committing any one of a number of what the rulebook calls 'palpably unfair acts', including kneeing or kicking an opponent, striking him with the fists, or flagrant roughing of the passer or kicker.

DIVE   A straight-ahead play into the line with the quarterback handing to the diving back. No faking is involved.

DOUBLE COVERAGE   This refers to a pass defense situation where a fast wide receiver is too good to be handled by one man. The defense will assign two men to the coverage.

DOUBLE FOUL   A rule infraction by both teams on the same down.

DOWN   The period of action starting when the ball is put in play and ending when it is dead.

DRAW PLAY   The quarterback fades back as if to pass but hands-off to the back who is pretending to block for the pass. This back, after a momentary delay in which he still retains the blocking stance, runs through any opening that presents itself.

DROPKICK   A type of kick in which the ball is dropped and kicked just as it rebounds from the ground.

EATING THE BALL   This is slang for describing what the quarterback does when he can't get a pass away. He keeps the ball and hides it as best he can about his person.

ELIGIBLE RECEIVER   The two ends and all four backs are eligible to receive a pass. This includes the quarterback, but he can't toss a pass to himself, so we are referring to the flankerback, left halfback and right halfback.

ENCROACHMENT   Movement by a player, usually a lineman, across the neutral zone before the snap. Contact with an opposing player occurs.

Defending against a field goal

END AROUND   A reverse in which the quarterback hands-off to an end who carries the ball around the opposite end. In most reverses the ball is given to a back.

END LINES   The lines at each end of the field.

END ZONES   The areas at each end of the field bounded by the end lines, sidelines, and goal lines.

ENDS   The two men that are lined up at either end of the offensive line. Usually one of these is close to the other linemen (a tight end) and the other is split away from them (the split end).

EXTRA POINT   The one-play, one-point conversion opportunity given to the team scoring a touchdown.

FACE GUARDING   This came from basketball. The defensive back may not obstruct the view of the receiver by placing his hands in the line of sight.

FACEMASKING   This is where the defense grabs the facemask to tackle a runner. It is very dangerous and as a result is carefully watched for by the officials.

FADE BACK   The term used to describe the quarterback dropping away from the line of scrimmage to throw a pass.

FAIR CATCH   An unhindered catch (of a kick) by a member of the receiving team. He must raise one arm full length above his head while the kick is in flight.

FAKE   A feigned action or play, usually by the quarterback, to confuse the defense.

FIELD GOAL   Three points, earned when a place kick goes over the crossbar and between the uprights (extended indefinitely upward) of the goal posts.

FILL   When a back hits a blocking assignment on the line, he is 'filling in' for the lineman.

FIRST DOWN   A team has four downs in which to gain ten yards. A 'first down' is earned when it gains a sufficient number of yards to be entitled to another sequence of four downs.

FLANKER   Another name for a wingback. Sometimes called a set back if coming from the same side of the backfield.

FLAT   The area either side of the line outside of the ends and in front of the cornerbacks.

FORWARD PASS   A ball thrown toward the opposing goal line.

FOUL   Any violation of a playing rule.

> 'We were so poor that when my mother threw a bone to our dog, he had to signal for a "fair catch", or us kids would beat him to it.'
>
> 'POOR BOY' STORY FROM WISCONSIN

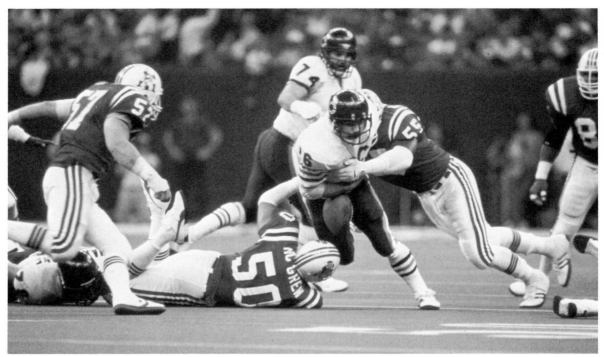

The fumble (above); *hand-off* (below)

FREE KICK   A play in which the defensive team is restrained from interfering with the kicker. It can occur as a kick-off, kick after a safety, or kick after a fair catch. It can take the form of a place kick, drop kick, or punt (except that a punt cannot be used on a kick-off).

FUMBLE   A ball in play after having been dropped or otherwise mishandled.

GOAL LINE   The line that separates the field of play from the end zone. There are goal lines 10 yards from and parallel to each of the end lines.

GOALPOST   Either of the two Y-shaped upright poles at each end of the field. The uprights themselves are $18\frac{1}{2}$ feet apart and connected by a crossbar 10 feet above the ground.

GRIDIRON   The name originally given to the field because the markings resembled those of a griddle or grill.

HALF-TIME   The fifteen-minute intermission between halves of a game.

HAND-OFF   The exchange of the ball from one offensive player to another.

HASHMARKS   The lines marking the central strip of the field lengthwise. All plays begin inside the marks, along the line of scrimmage.

HUDDLE   The grouping of the offense, prior to a play. The play and starting signal are given by the quarterback.

ILLEGAL PROCEDURE   Movement on the part of a member of the offensive line after the team is set but before the ball is snapped.

IN-BOUNDS LINES   The two series of short lines that run the length of the field. Each is 70 feet 9 inches from the near sideline. (See Hashmarks.)

INCOMPLETION   A forward pass that is not completed.

INELIGIBLE RECEIVER   An offensive player, normally an interior tackle, guard, or centre, not permitted to catch a forward pass.

IN MOTION   An offensive player, not on the line, who is allowed to run laterally before the snap.

INTENTIONAL GROUNDING   An infraction of the rules in which a passer deliberately throws an incomplete pass in order to avoid being tackled behind the line of scrimmage.

INTERCEPTION   A pass caught by a defensive player.

INTERFERENCE   Offensive players blocking in front of the ball carrier.

INTERIOR LINEMEN   Five offensive players (two tackles, two guards, one centre) who form the middle of the scrimmage line of seven men.

Incompletion

Pass rush, a defensive lineman pursuing the quarterback

KEYING Refers to the defensive player observing the movements of a certain offensive man to get a clue or 'key' as to where the play will be going.

KICKING TEE A plastic device on which to place the ball prior to kicking.

KICK-OFF A place kick used to begin play at the start of a half or after a score.

LATERAL A pass that travels to either side or backwards.

LINE OF SCRIMMAGE The imaginary line from sideline to sideline which separates the offense and defense at the beginning of each play.

LINEMAN One of the seven offensive players positioned at the line of scrimmage - the centre, two guards, two tackles, and two ends.

LIVE BALL A ball legally free-kicked or snapped.

LOOSE BALL A ball in play not in possession of any player.

MAN-TO-MAN A pass defense assigning defenders the responsibility of covering specific receivers.

MUFF To touch a loose ball in an unsuccessful attempt to gain possession.

MULTIPLE FOUL Two or more fouls by the same team on the same down.

NEUTRAL ZONE The area between the offensive and defensive lines of scrimmage. It is the length of the ball in width.

NOSE GUARD The defensive player positioned in front of the centre's nose.

OFFENSE The team in possesion of the ball.

OFFENSIVE HOLDING Illegal use of the hands while blocking a defensive player.

OFFICIAL Any one of the members of the seven-man officiating team regulating play and enforcing the rules.

OFF-SETTING PENALTIES A situation occurring when both teams are guilty of rule infractions on the same down. The penalties cancel each other out.

OFFSIDE Occurs when any part of a player's body is beyond his scrimmage or free-kick line when the ball is snapped.

ONSIDE The side toward which the play is run.

ONSIDE KICK A short kick-off by means of which the kicking team hopes to retain possession of the ball.

PASS INTERFERENCE Illegal interference with a player's opportunity to catch a forward pass or make an interception.

PENALTY MARKER The handkerchief-sized yellow flag carried by an official and thrown to the ground to indicate a rule violation.

PERSONAL FOUL An instance of illegal hitting, such as unnecessary roughness, clipping, piling on, kicking, punching, or running into the passer or kicker.

PILING ON Falling upon or throwing oneself upon a downed ball carrier after the whistle has sounded.

PLACE KICK A kick executed while the ball is in a fixed position on the ground, either on a tee or held by a teammate.

PLACEMENT A place kick.

PLAY ACTION PASS A run is faked but the quarterback keeps the ball and passes.

POCKET The protected area formed by the five interior linemen in which the quarterback sets up to throw.

'There's nothing that cleanses your soul like getting the hell kicked out of you.'

WOODY HAYES
OHIO STATE

Setting up the pass pocket

POSSESSION   A rulebook term that refers to any player who holds and controls the ball long enough 'to perform any act common to the game'.

PUNT   A kick from scrimmage made when a player drops the ball and kicks it while it is in the air.

PUNT RETURN   The runback of a punt.

QUARTER   One of the four fifteen-minute periods that constitute a game.

QUICK KICK   This kick goes from a normal running or passing formation. It is usually called on third down when the defense is not expecting it. The ball is kicked flat so that it will go low and hopefully have a long roll. (You seldom see this in the pro game.)

> 'They say I teach brutal football, but the only thing brutal about football is losing.'
>
> BEAR BRYANT, COACH, ALABAMA

RECOVER   To gain possession of a fumbled ball.

RED DOG   A rush by a defensive back to get to the quarterback before he can release the pass.

RETURN   A runback of a kick, punt, or an intercepted pass.

ROLL OUT PASS   (Sprint Pass) Instead of dropping back into the pass pocket, the quarterback runs right or left looking for a receiver. If none materializes, he might 'throw the ball away' or run with it himself. (See photograph on page 106.)

ROUGHING THE KICKER   To run into the kicker in a violent manner.

RUSHING   Running with the ball on a play from scrimmage.

SACK   To tackle or otherwise down the quarterback for a loss while he is attempting to pass.

SAFETY   A situation in which the ball is dead on or behind a team's own goal, with the impetus coming from a player on that team. Two points are awarded to the opposing team.

Roll-out or sprint pass

SCREEN PASS   The defensive linemen are allowed to rush the quarterback who encourages them by fading deep. In the meantime a receiver positions himself behind the screen of blockers formed by the offensive linemen. The quarterback throws over the heads of the rushing defensive linemen and the receiver now has an escort of blockers to clear his path.

SHIFT   The movement of two or more offensive players at the same time before the snap.

SHOTGUN   An offensive formation in which the quarterback moves to the tailback spot and takes the old-fashioned long snap from the centre.

SIDELINES   The line at each side of the field extending from end line to end line.

SLOT BACK   A backfield man positioned just off the line of scrimmage in a slot or gap created by splitting the end. Here he can block for the run and be in position for a reverse while at the same time being in a good pass-receiving position.

SNAP   The passing of the football from the centre to the quarterback.

SPEARING   An attempt by one player to hurt or injure another by lungeing at him helmet-first.

STRIPPING   Taking the ball away from the carrier while tackling him high.

STUNTS   Manoeuvres used by defensive men to confuse the blockers and cause them to miss their assignments. The defensive equivalent of a trap.

SUDDEN DEATH   The continuation of a tied game into overtime. The team scoring first (by safety, field goal, or touchdown) wins.

SWEEP   A running play going wide around the end. (Power Sweep is the same, but with pulling linemen and backs leading the play).

SWING PASS   A short pass to a back who loops or 'swings' outside of the end but still behind the line of scrimmage.

> 'I never make a tackle just to bring someone down. I want to punish the man I'm going after, and I want him to know that it's going to hurt everytime he comes my way.'
>
> JACK TATUM,
> OAKLAND RAIDERS

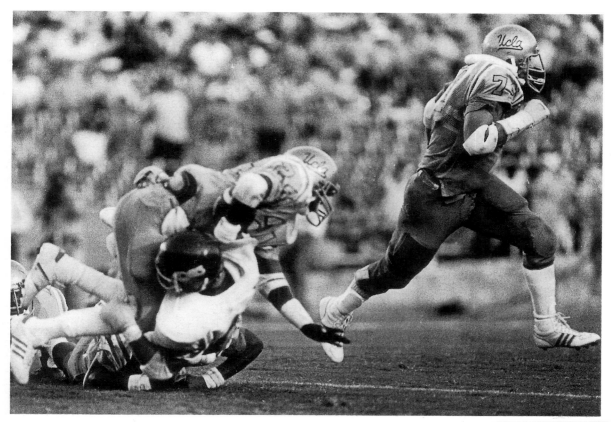

Tackle - successful (above) *and unsuccessful* (right)

TACKLING   The act of bringing down the ball carrier.

TAILBACK   A backfield man lined up directly behind the centre from five to seven yards deep.

TIME-OUT   An interval during the game when play is not legally in progress and the official clock is stopped.

TOUCHBACK   Occurs when any kick touches anything while the ball is on or behind the receiver's goal line. The team whose goal line is involved puts the ball in play on its own 20-yard line.

TOUCHDOWN   Occurs (a) when a runner advances the ball so that it touches or crosses the opponents' goal line or (b) when a ball is caught or recovered by a player while it is on or behind his opponents' goal line.

TRAP   A play in which a defensive lineman is allowed to come through the line and then is blocked from the side.

TRIPLE-THREAT MAN   A backfield man who can run, pass and kick equally well – the kick would be a 'quick kick'. This kind of player is seldom seen in today's specialized game where individual assignments are the norm.

TRY-FOR-POINT   The opportunity given the team scoring a touchdown to add another point by successfully executing a single play from scrimmage. The ball is put in play from the two-yard line.

TURNOVER   Loss of the ball to the opponents by a fumble or pass interception.

TWO-MINUTE OFFENSE   Designed for the last minutes of the game when a score is needed and all time-outs have been used. Since time is precious, none is wasted in huddling between downs. The team lines up quickly and the quarterback calls the play by using audibles.

TWO-MINUTE WARNING   Official's verbal notification to the head coaches that two minutes of playing time remain in the half.

TWO POINT OPTION   In college or high school football, a team scoring a touchdown has the option of trying for either one or two points. The ball is placed on the two-yard line. A team is awarded one point for a successful place kick, or two points for successfully running or passing the ball across the goal line.

WIDE RECEIVER   A backfield man positioned just off the line and ten yards or more outside the offensive end position.

WINGBACK   A backfield man positioned just off the line and immediately outside his offensive end. His duties are the same as that of the slot back. He is sometimes called a set back or flanker.

YARD LINE   Any of the lines marked at five-yard intervals across the field of play between the two goal lines.

YARDAGE   Distance lost or gained by the offensive team on a play from scrimmage.

ZONE DEFENSE   Pass defense making defenders responsible for covering a specific area of the field.

> 'I've got nothing to say and I'll only say it once.'
>
> DARRELL ROYAL,
> TEXAS FOOTBALL COACH,
> AFTER LOSING A CLOSE GAME